A division of

D1471912

The Estates Gazette
1 Procter Street, London WC1V 6EU

Typeset by Amy Boyle, Rochester, Kent
Printed and bound by Bell & Bain Ltd., Glasgow

# Contents

# Table of Legislation and Regulations

## Regulations

# European Directives

# List of Tables and Figures

## Tables

## Figures

# Foreword

As I write, a family member is dying of mesothelioma, and a former colleague has recently died of it. Neither had worked in the asbestos industry, and their minor asbestos exposure had seemed unimportant when it happened. Although this is devastating for the two victims and their close families, statistically it is not at all surprising. Roughly one percent of my age group of men in Britain will die of asbestos-related disease, and many, perhaps most, will have been unaware of any significant exposure. We cannot do anything about these past exposures, but if we have personal contact with victims we will feel that any measure is justified to stop it happening in future.

But there is another side. I am a trustee of a charity responsible for a range of buildings of various ages. Some certainly contain asbestos. Every penny and minute we spend on surveys and management plans is instead of what we feel we should be doing. For fellow trustees and hard-pressed staff this is a tiresome and expensive bureaucratic obstruction with no obvious benefit, and it is not surprising that I sometimes have an uphill job persuading people of its importance.

In the middle of this are asbestos surveyors. Their thoroughness and skill may save the lives of people they will never meet, and certainly their ability to do their job efficiently and economically is going to be financially important for their clients.

So this book is important to all these people. Bill Sanderson is unsurpassed in Britain in his combined experience of surveying, training surveyors, and involvement in development of key HSE guidance and UKAS accreditation. I think that this book will immediately become a standard work used for training surveyors, and dog-eared copies will soon be found with the copies of the HSE publications in many surveyors' cars.

But if you agree with me, you will have probably skipped the Foreword to get to the real contents. If you are still with me, let me thank you on behalf of the people you will never meet, who will probably never realise that an asbestos surveyor helped save their life!

*Trevor Ogden*

Dr Trevor Ogden was for many years the HSE's leading authority on asbestos testing methods and procedures in the Health and Safety Laboratory at Cricklewood. He was chair of the Committee on Fibre Management, and later head of HSE's Asbestos Policy Section. He was chair of the Working Group for Asbestos Testing for NAMAS in the early stages of laboratory accreditation. Over the last few years he has chaired the ABICS Management Committee, developing the formation of one of the schemes to certify individual asbestos surveyors.

# Introduction

Asbestos has been used on an industrial scale in the United Kingdom since the latter part of the 19th century. As a result, asbestos-related diseases in the UK have grown over the course of the 20th century to become the biggest cause of industrial disease and deaths after accidents. Over the last two decades, the death rate from mesothelioma in particular seems to have accelerated alarmingly – far beyond the expectations of the Health and Safety Executive (HSE) only 20 years ago. This death rate is now predicted to continue increasing until somewhere between 2010 and 2015, although it is very unclear how fast the death rate will decline after the peak.

Records to 2001 show at least 25,000 deaths from mesothelioma since 1975. When asbestosis and lung cancer associated with asbestos are taken into account, the total number of deaths has certainly exceeded 50,000. The sad fact is that each of these is a personal and painful tragedy, and each death could, and should, have been prevented.

In the industrial age, the first indications of a health problem in the UK were already highlighted in about 1898 by a lady inspector of factories, drawing attention to evidence of ill health among factory workers in the asbestos manufacturing industry. This situation was emphasized in a further report in 1906, where deaths were clearly linked to asbestos exposure.

Despite the introduction of the first legislation – the Asbestos Industries Regulations 1931 – the asbestos industry continued to promote and develop its products. Imports of raw asbestos peaked in the mid 1970s when about 170,000 tons were being imported each year, although amphibole asbestos (amosite and crocidolite) imports declined rapidly after 1969 when evidence of mesothelioma became well established.

Total imports of asbestos into the UK in the 20th century are estimated to amount to about six million tons, mostly chrysotile. The vast majority of this was used in a wide range of building products, estimated as 3,000 applications of asbestos. Although asbestos removal has been active since the late 1970s very substantial amounts of asbestos containing materials are still found in the stock of older buildings. Consequently, when maintenance activities disturb these materials, staff such as carpenters, electricians and plumbers are particularly liable to be exposed to airborne asbestos when inadequately protected.

The HSE considered that most asbestos related deaths occurred in the manufacturing and major installation activities, such as lagging in power stations. In the mid 1980s, they were expecting mesothelioma deaths to reach a peak in the early 1990s and then decline – because crocidolite had effectively been withdrawn from use by a voluntary trade ban on its import and use in 1969. They were appalled when Professor Julian Peto reviewed the figures in 1995 (Peto, Hodgson, Matthews, Jones, *Lancet* 1995; **345**: pp 535–539) and showed that mesothelioma deaths would continue to increase, possibly not peaking until 2020 and that asbestos related deaths could double or treble by then. In 1985, mesothelioma deaths were about 600 per year when the HSE made its prediction, about 1250 per year when Peto carried out his review, but had already reached 1850 per year by 2001.

Peto also clearly identified that 25% of cases in the mid-1990s were from people who had worked in the building trades. With hindsight – a wonderful thing, to be sure – it is clear the HSE had underestimated the effects of "casual" exposures from maintenance activities. Because of the durability of the inhaled fibres – particularly for the amphiboles – cumulative exposures are clearly very significant, particularly with poorly controlled conditions. Maintenance workers may be unaware of the materials they are disturbing or have rather cavalier attitudes because older staff will have worked for many years with these materials, perhaps installing them in the first place. The implication was that unless anything was done actively to prevent the exposures continuing, the death rates would continue to increase.

The first response by the HSE was a comment in the Consultative Document CD127 in 1998, when the Asbestos (Licensing) Regulations 1983 were being amended to include for the first time a statutory requirement to hold a licence from the HSE for work on asbestos insulating board (AIB). The HSE indicated that they were considering revising the Control of Asbestos at Work Regulations (CAWR) 1987 to include a general duty to manage asbestos in premises to prevent accidental exposures and to keep any asbestos in good condition. The duty would not exclude the removal of asbestos but the objective was clearly to prevent unnecessary exposure to asbestos by either maintenance workers or other people in the building. (One of the problems may be that the younger maintenance trades people will not have worked with these materials and may therefore find it difficult to recognise them in the workplace.)

The new "duty to manage asbestos in non-domestic premises" was formally proposed in CD159 in May 2000, but the original consultation raised problems with the definition of the "dutyholder" in complex tenancy or leasehold situations. It therefore had to be re-consulted in CD176 in December 2001 and was not finally laid before Parliament until September 2002. There were some alarms because of a challenge by the Conservative opposition, galvanised by a lobby group from the Asbestos Cement Manufacturers Association. When the debate in the House of Commons was proposed, the old 1987 Control of Asbestos at Work Regulations had already been revoked and if the Opposition amendment had been carried, we could have been left without any Control of Asbestos at Work Regulations at all – an alarming situation!

The danger passed – but not before an excellent debate in the House of Lords – and the regulations duly became law on 21 November 2002. The regulations provided for an 18-month lead-in period to allow dutyholders time to comply with the new duty to manage – Regulation 4. By 21 May 2004, dutyholders must have had adequate management plans to control asbestos in non-domestic premises. Although the HSE have mounted a substantial campaign to bring the new regulations to the attention of industry – and to explain what needs to be done – the evidence is that many companies passed the deadline without having comprehended the new regulation, let alone having an adequate management plan in place. By early summer 2004, the HSE were making it plain that they planned to inspect large organisations, industry and local authorities, to assess their compliance with the new regulation.

The first necessity is for the dutyholder to assess whether asbestos containing materials are likely to be present in the building fabric and, if so, to establish good records – by a survey if necessary – and to assess the condition of any ACMs (*a*sbestos *c*ontaining *m*aterials) located.

It must be emphasized that surveying buildings for asbestos materials is highly dependent on experience. When learning surveying there can be no substitute for seeing ACMs in the building components where they have been used, and surveyors need to experience a range of building types and ages. Often the ACMs have been used for good technical reasons, but sometimes there seems to be no explanation as to why an asbestos material was used. Experienced surveyors may still find a novel material used in a particular manner they have never seen before.

This book, therefore, is intended to be a guide to surveyors on the technical aspects of asbestos, the types of materials to be found and why it was originally used. It is hoped to indicate where it could be found in buildings, to indicate what type of survey is required and how to undertake it. Lastly, we need to understand what information the surveyor needs to give the dutyholder for them to compile an adequate management plan.

The duty of care incumbent on the asbestos surveyor is evident. As for any survey, the various consequences of an incompetent or inadequate survey are very substantial. The rush of work to produce the required number of surveys is in danger of producing poor quality surveys and the HSE are looking very carefully at some of the outcomes. They will not hesitate to prosecute an incompetent surveyor and the client will obviously seek to gain some redress.

It is therefore essential that surveyors are properly trained with the appropriate field experience. Building surveyors will have the appropriate surveying and inspection techniques, but asbestos is a highly specialist area and it is important for them to have the relevant information to be able to carry out the survey and assessment effectively to enable the client (the dutyholder under regulation 4 of the Control of Asbestos at Work Regulations 2002) to discharge their responsibilities fully and effectively.

Surveyors should look carefully at the possibility of certification under ISO/IEC 17024 or accreditation as an Inspection Body under ISO/IEC 17020. Although not required at the time of writing this book, the HSE have made it plain that certification or accreditation may be introduced as a requirement of the Control of Asbestos at Work Regulations when they are revised in 2005.

# Legislation on Asbestos

## Health and Safety at Work etc Act 1974

The Health and Safety at Work etc Act 1974 (HSWA 1974) is the principal piece of legislation to consider. It was introduced following the Robens Commission under a Labour Government, but it was completed and enacted under the next Conservative administration. It has undoubtedly been the single most influential piece of legislation on health and safety in the workplace. Although it is now 30 years old, it is still a very effective and useful Act. It was intended to be a goal setting – putting into place procedures by which health and safety should be managed pro-actively. In effect, it provides a comprehensive structure for the management of health and safety in the workplace as well as its oversight and enforcement by the Health and Safety Executive (HSE) with orders, and ultimately with prosecution through the courts.

One of its major features – an illustration of the power and influence enjoyed by the trade unions in the 1970s – is the prominence given to the rights and duties of the employee in the workplace. Before this, the regulations and Acts dealing with health and safety were directed principally at the employer with little involvement of the employee. Now, although the major duties remain with the employer, the employee had for the first time, rights of access to information, safety training, representation and consultation about safety management (section 2).

The other side of the coin, however, was the duty (section 7) on the individual to take due care and attention for their own safety as well as the safety of others who may be affected by what they do, or fail to do. This is no empty threat. There have been many prosecutions of individuals under section 7.

Clearly the industrial landscape in the UK has changed dramatically in the last three decades with the loss of so much heavy industry and with a switch to the service economy, and much reduced influence and power of the trade unions. The HSWA could well be revisited to bring it up to date and this has been considered although overtaken by other political priorities.

Not only the industrial landscape, but also the role of the Health and Safety Commission as a policy-making body has changed. Health and safety matters, as in so many other spheres, now are driven very largely by European Directives. The structure of the HSWA, however, gives a means of introducing new legislation to implement new directives. One of the exceptions to this rule was the introduction of the new regulation 4, the duty to manage asbestos in non-domestic premises in the Control of Asbestos at Work Regulations 2002 (CAWR). Although some European countries have a similar, if not equivalent, regulation on their statute books, (Holland, Belgium and France, for example), this was driven by a domestic, not European, agenda.

## Summaries of European Directives and UK Regulations

| *European Directive* | *UK Regulation* |
|---|---|
| 83/477/EEC | Control of Asbestos at Work Regulations 1987 |
| 91/659/EEC | Asbestos (Prohibitions) Regulations 1992 |
| 1999/77/EC | Asbestos (Prohibitions) (Amendment) Regulations 1999 |
| 1999/77/EC | Asbestos (Prohibitions) (Amendment) Regulations 2003 |
| – | Control of Asbestos at Work Regulations 2002 |
| 2003/18/EC | Control of Asbestos at Work (Amendment) Regulations 2005? |

The HSWA 1974 is referred to as an "enabling" Act, since it gives powers to the Secretary of State to prepare regulations to implement the provisions of the Act with regard to a range of hazards and ensuring a safe workplace. Since 1974, several dozen regulations – some amended more than once – have been produced under this Act. With enabling Acts, Parliament spends a great deal of energy and time getting the Act right, and the regulations follow with relatively little discussion in Parliament. In most cases, the new regulation in the form of an SI or Statutory Instrument is laid before Parliament and is automatically put on the Statute Book, provided there is no objection in the House of Commons.

No new regulations or approved codes of practice (ACoP) can be issued, however, without due consultation (sections 15 and 16 HSWA) and the HSE are duty-bound to take note of what people say in response. The process now is very accessible through the HSE website, www.hse.gov.uk. Consultative documents are free from HSE Books www.hsebooks.co.uk or from the HSE website and responses can be submitted by e-mail to the appropriate person in HSE Policy. The HSE later issues a summary of the responses taken into consideration in the consultation process.

From the surveyor's point of view, it is clearly important to recognise that the employer has a duty to maintain a safe workplace that does not expose employees and others to risks to their health (HSWA sections 2 and 3). This extends (section 4) also to others who use the premises, as tenants or sub-let premises, where the landlord is in control of the premises and is responsible for the repair and maintenance. This is the starting point for regulation 4 of the CAWR 2002 – the duty to manage asbestos in non-domestic premises.

The duty on the surveyor to do his work safely and competently is found in section 7 – general duties on employees at work. Section 36 (and section 37 for corporate bodies) allows for any person, whose negligence or incompetence causes another person to commit an offence under any regulation, to be charged with that offence themselves, regardless of whether the other person is charged or not.

It is significant that an example of this has already occurred in 1998 as a result of a superficial and incompetent survey where some obvious asbestos was missed in a demolition survey and later disturbed by the demolition contractor. It was the survey company that was prosecuted and fined a total of £43,000 including costs. This prosecution was for a survey of a CDM (Construction (Design and Management) Regulations 1994) redevelopment project at a former hospital. To be fair, this is just one of several similar prosecutions brought by the HSE since 1998 and recorded on the prosecutions database on the HSE website: case no F100000282. There are at least 11 other similar convictions recorded, with total fines and costs awarded to the HSE of £192,000 at an average of £16,000 per case.

# ACoP

ACoPs are approved (after consultation) by the Health and Safety Commission as guidance on what an employer would be required to do in order to comply with regulations. They are written and issued by the HSE and are detailed and helpful indications of what is required. Although not statutory requirements – and only the courts can interpret the regulations – they are used in the case of a prosecution to determine whether a regulation had been complied with. The defendant's case – and the burden of proof of innocence rests on the defendant – could be that what he or she did was at least as good as the requirement of the ACoP; that they had complied with the regulation in another equally good way; or that it was not reasonably practicable to comply with the regulation (if that is a defence) in the first place.

There are at present three sets of ACoP relating to the CAWR 2002:

## L27 Work with asbestos which does not normally require a licence

This covers minor work on asbestos materials, including the work of surveyors and analysts, sampling bulk materials for an asbestos survey and air sampling for asbestos for any purposes (clearance sampling after asbestos removal, reassurance sampling or sampling for personal exposure records where medical records are required to be kept). It replaces the old general approved code of practice which was addressed mainly at the manufacturing industry, now effectively extinct.

## L28 Work with asbestos insulation, asbestos coating and asbestos insulating board

These are the procedures to be followed by licensed asbestos removal contractors (or employers with their own staff on their premises) when working on these materials. It is clearly important for both client and contractor to be aware of the procedures to be followed when asbestos removal or repair works are being undertaken.

## L127 The duty to manage asbestos in non-domestic premises

The new regulation 4 in CAWR 2002 has its own ACoP. The regulation is very comprehensive and even though the regulation had a lead-in period of 18 months, many duty holders would have struggled to achieve any level of compliance within the given period.

When the regulations came into force, the HSE made it quite clear that if a serious incident with asbestos occurred before 21 May 2004, where it was deemed that management controls had failed, the HSE would have had no hesitation in prosecuting under the Management of Health and Safety at Work Regulations 1999 (MHSAW).

## HSE guidance

In addition to the regulations and ACoP, there is specific guidance issued by the HSE for work in specific industries, mostly as Environmental Health (EH) Guidance Notes or now, more commonly, as HSG guidance notes. Some of the more important ones are/were:

| | |
|---|---|
| EH 10 | Asbestos: exposure limits and measurement of airborne dust concentrations |
| EH 47 | Provision, use and maintenance of hygiene facilities for work with asbestos insulation, asbestos coating and asbestos insulating board** |
| EH 50 | Training operatives and supervisors for work with asbestos insulation and asbestos coatings ** |
| EH 51 | Enclosures provided for work with asbestos insulation, coatings and asbestos insulating board ** |
| EH 57 | Problems with asbestos removal at high temperatures (now withdrawn) |
| HSG 189/1 | Controlled asbestos stripping techniques for work requiring a licence** |

HSG 189/2            Working with asbestos cement
HSG 210 and 213 Asbestos Essentials and Introduction to Asbestos
                          Essentials

It should be noted many of these (**) are due to be replaced by the
"Licensed Contractor's Guide" which will appear in late 2004. The
HSE are taking the opportunity to consolidate recommendations on
best practice and to move standards forward.

Guidance documents do not have the same legal or enforcement
status as the ACoP, of course, but are recommended as best practice
by the HSE.

# Methods for the Determination of Hazardous Substances

The Methods for the Determination of Hazardous Substances
(MDHS) series includes specific and general methods developed and
issued by the HSE for the sampling and analysis of a range of
workplace hazardous materials. Some analytes could be sampled
and measured by a number of different techniques, and in some
cases (eg MDHS 100) the MDHS deals less with the analysis and
more with the surveying and sampling of the materials.

The standard methods for various aspects of asbestos sampling
and analysis are:

MDHS 39/4   **Asbestos fibres in air** (Sampling and evaluation by
                  Phase Contrast Optical Microscopy (PCM))
MDHS 77      **Asbestos in bulk materials** (Sampling and
                  identification by polarised light microscopy (PLM))
MDHS 87      **Fibres in air** (Guidance on the discrimination
                  techniques for fibre counting of airborne fibres)
MDHS 100     **Surveying, sampling and assessment of asbestos-
                  containing materials**

Many laboratories will also be familiar with:

MDHS 59      **Man-made mineral fibre** (Air sampling and fibre
                  counting for MMMF by optical phase contrast
                  microscopy)

MDHS 39/4 remains the formal air sampling and fibre counting method to be used until the European Directive 2003/18/EC is implemented when CAWR 2002 is amended, probably late in 2005. From January 2006, HSE will expect asbestos clearances to be done by the method in Annex I of the Analysts Guide. This method implements the World Health Organization (WHO) fibre counting rules as recommended in the European Directive. MDHS 59 for sampling and fibre counting of Man made Mineral Fibre (MMMF) also will remain, but eventually will be replaced by Annex I in the Analysts Guide.

MDHS 77 for the identification of asbestos in bulk samples (see chapter 10) will also appear in the Analysts Guide as Annex II (but may not include the sampling techniques referred to in MDHS 77).

MDHS 100 is clearly the definitive document that surveyors must adhere to. It includes illustrations of a range of typical and not so typical asbestos materials and defines the types of surveys now common parlance in the trade. It was suggested that this MDHS was not a true analytical method and therefore did not belong in this series. Nevertheless, this is where it stands and, as far as the surveyor and the client are concerned, this is the standard reference document.

As a general rule, MDHS methods are procedures that have been developed and validated by the HSE and are recommended practice. They are not mandatory but, in some cases, (eg MDHS 39/4 for airborne asbestos fibre sampling and counting) an analyst would need to demonstrate clearly that any other procedure or deviation from the MDHS can produce a result with at least the same validity and confidence.

Accreditation by United Kingdom Accreditation Service (UKAS) to the appropriate standard (ISO/IEC 17025 or 17020 (see chapter 3)) would require recognised published procedures to be followed. For asbestos, MDHS 39/4 (or its successor) and MDHS 77 do not constitute analytical and sampling procedures in themselves. An accredited organisation would therefore need to supplement these with "documented in-house procedures".

# Enforcement actions

The HSE's inspectors have very significant powers of enforcement if they deem a regulation or regulations are not being complied with.

Their powers of entry into premises (if necessary accompanied by a police officer), taking samples and evidence, taking witness statements, copies of documentation are described in section 20 of HSWA 1974.

# Improvement notices

Where an inspector finds that a regulation is not being complied with, he can issue an improvement notice, requiring the employer to remedy the situation within a specified period. The inspector must specify which piece of legislation is being contravened (and in what instance) but does not need to specify what measures must be taken to remedy the contravention – although he may offer options and refer to an appropriate approved code of practice.

As an example of improvement notices, prior to the introduction of CAWR 2002 and the new duty to manage asbestos in premises, the HSE visited a number of local authorities to assess their state of knowledge of the asbestos in their corporate, commercial and domestic buildings. If they were not happy that the authority had adequate records, the HSE issued improvement notices – under the MHSAW 1999. These regulations require an employer to make an adequate assessment of all risks at work to his employees and to anyone who may be affected by the hazard.

# Prohibition notices

Prohibition notices would be issued where the inspector is of the opinion that there is an immediate danger or risk to personal safety. The notice can take effect immediately or at a given point in time. Again, the inspector must give details of the risk concerned and his reasons for the notice. This notice can be issued to the person in charge of the site and not necessarily to the managing director who may be many miles away and not directly in charge of the works.

The prohibition notice would have the effect of stopping a specific activity. It would not necessarily close a whole site, of course.

# Appeals

An employer can appeal against either an improvement or prohibition notice to an industrial tribunal. This has the effect of suspending the notice until the appeal has been heard and disposed of, but, in the case of a prohibition notice, the suspension is at the discretion of the tribunal.

# Prosecutions

As a last resort, the inspectors may prosecute where gross violations of the HSWA 1974 or of the associated regulations are found. The prosecution may be taken against a range of parties, including the client and individual employees. In a recent case (2000) at a motorway services, where asbestos ceiling tiles were incompetently and dangerously removed, the HSE prosecuted all the parties involved: the client, the planning supervisor, the principal contractor, the asbestos removal contractor and the analytical company. All were convicted and the fines totalled over £180,000. It cannot have helped the client's case that he had a previous conviction for a very similar offence at the same site just two years previously: see HSE website case no F120000369.

# HSE inspectors

Prosecutions are just the end of the road. The role of the inspector is to try and ensure that the regulations are complied with in the first place. Most inspectors will be very helpful if asked for advice and assistance. They may not be able to give definitive answers over the phone without seeing the particular situation but may be able to point out sources of information. As a general principle, it is worth cultivating a good relationship with your friendly inspector!

The HSE publishes a wide range of excellent and accessible documentation (at very reasonable prices, compared with British Standards, for example) to try and help employers as much as possible. The standard of presentation in HSE documents has improved out of all recognition over the last decade.

9

# "Practicable" and "reasonably practicable"

There are three levels of requirements in the safety legislation:

1. An absolute requirement to do or not do something as the case may be. This is not negotiable.
2. "So far as is practicable" decrees that the requirement should be fulfilled where there is the time, the technology and the capability to do or not do something.
3. "So far as is reasonably practicable" permits an employer to take into account the cost and difficulty of doing something to counter a risk. However, unless there is a gross disproportion between the cost, time and difficulty on the one hand and the degree of risk on the other (and it can be shown that the risk is insignificant in relation to the cost), the employer should take appropriate precautions and incur the necessary cost.

The phrase "so far as is reasonably practicable" occurs frequently in the legislation and guidance but the precise interpretation would ultimately be up to the courts to decide in each case.

# Control of Asbestos at Work Regulations 2002

Control of Asbestos at Work Regulations 2002 (CAWR) replaces all its predecessors, the Control of Asbestos at Work Regulations 1987 (as amended 1992 and 1998), which themselves replaced the Asbestos Industries Regulations 1931 and the Asbestos Regulations 1969.

The Asbestos Industries Regulations 1931 were introduced as a response to the growing evidence of asbestos-related disease but were aimed at the processing and manufacturing rather than the installation or maintenance activities. Likewise, the Asbestos Regulations 1969 were introduced in response to the new information in the 1950s on lung cancer and, particularly, on mesothelioma. An interesting aspect of the 1969 regulations was that for the first time they introduced the requirement to notify the factory inspector 28 days before beginning any work (including removal) involving crocidolite. (Although these regulations have been entirely superseded, this notification requirement lives on in the folk-memory and is often a cause of confusion in people who are not up to date with asbestos legislation.)

The Control of Asbestos at Work Regulations 1987 were introduced to implement the European Directive 83/477/EEC, on the Protection of Workers from Asbestos. It contained the European Reference Method (ERM) with the fibre counting definitions, which became the basis of MDHS 39 in its successive editions. MDHS 39/4 included the ERM as the "Approved Method" as Annex I (although in earlier versions, the ERM was included in HSE's Guidance Note EH10). CAWR 1987 was amended in 1992 and again in 1998 before being replaced entirely by CAWR 2002.

CAWR 2002 are the principal regulations relating to work on asbestos materials and the intention here is to describe the requirements, but only in sufficient detail to appreciate the objectives of this legislation. For precise information and interpretation it is essential to refer to the actual legislation.

# Definitions

The regulations define the exposure limits in terms of "control limits" and "action levels". A control limit is a time-weighted average exposure over either a continuous four-hour period or a short-term 10-minute period. The relevant limit must not be exceeded unless the worker is protected by suitable respiratory protective equipment which will reduce the exposure as low as is reasonably practicable and in any case below the control limit. The action level, on the other hand, is a measure of an employee's cumulative exposure over a continuous 12-week working period; exceeding an action level will trigger a number of actions in the regulations.

# Risk assessments and plans of work

Before work commences, an employer should identify the type of asbestos (or assume it contains an amphibole), undertake a risk assessment, which should identify the control measures needed, and produce a plan of work. The plan of work must be kept at the site of work and must be followed as far as is reasonably practicable. If the exposure is liable to exceed any relevant action level, the work must be notified to the appropriate enforcing authority and employees will need to be under medical surveillance.

## Information, instruction and training

Persons (employees and others on the premises) liable to be exposed to asbestos must receive appropriate information, instruction and training at suitable intervals, at a level which is appropriate to their involvement with the work or the expected exposure. The employer should prevent or reduce to the lowest level practicable the exposure of his employees and others to asbestos, preferably by means other than the provision of respiratory protective equipment (RPE). If RPE is provided, it should be suitable and capable of reducing the exposure to a level as low as is reasonably practicable. The emphasis is on control measures and minimising the number of people exposed to asbestos.

## Control measures and maintenance

The employer must ensure that control measures are properly used and the employee must make full and proper use of them. Control measures must be properly maintained and records kept of testing, examination and any repairs to equipment such as vacuum cleaners, negative pressure units or hygiene units. Protective clothing must be cleaned at suitable intervals or disposed of as asbestos waste. There needs to be adequate arrangements to deal with incidents and emergencies.

## Duty to prevent the spread of asbestos

This is the shortest (and perhaps the most important) regulation. All work on friable asbestos materials (specifically asbestos insulation, asbestos coatings and asbestos insulating board) must be carried out with an enclosure.

# Cleanliness of premises

An employer (eg removal contractor) must leave the work premises thoroughly clean. The ACoP L28 gives specific guidance on procedures to be followed for clearance of enclosures before re-occupation.

# Air monitoring and asbestos identification

Employees exposed (or liable to be exposed) to asbestos above the action level must have that exposure monitored and recorded. Personal sampling results for a health surveillance record must be kept (together with the health surveillance record) for 40 years. Any air monitoring done must be either by an employer on his own premises (but in accordance with the standards in ISO 17025) or must be by an organisation accredited by UKAS as complying with ISO 17025. Likewise, the same standards will apply for laboratories carrying out asbestos identification from November 2004.

# Health records and surveillance

Employees exposed to asbestos above the action level must be under routine medical surveillance at intervals not less than two years while the exposure lasts, and have had a medical examination not more than two years before the beginning of such exposure. These records need to be kept for 40 years after the date of the last entry. The medical certificates are issued to both employer and employee. These are simply certificates of examination and do not necessarily certify that someone is "fit" to work with asbestos. Clearly, if evidence of an asbestos-related disease is detected, then the employer must consider providing alternative employment which does not expose the employee to asbestos.

# Washing and changing facilities

Employers must provide adequate hygiene facilities where employees are exposed to asbestos. This is an extension to the regulation on the prevention of the spread of asbestos.

The most important change in CAWR 2002 is, of course, the new "duty to manage asbestos in non-domestic premises" and this will be discussed in more detail in chapter 6. The consequent management plan will be discussed in chapter 12.

# Asbestos (Licensing) Regulations 1983 (amended 1998)

The Asbestos (Licensing) Regulations were issued at a time when there were a number of contractors doing a lot of removal work to (in some cases) extremely poor standards. The HSE felt it necessary to be able to keep track of the work contractors were doing.

Initially, the regulations covered only asbestos insulation and asbestos coatings. In 1983, the import of amosite, the production and installation of asbestos insulating board was still permitted and not legally prohibited until 1985. Asbestos Insulating Board (AIB) was not included under these regulations until 1998, although from 1992, the HSE recognised that "major" work with AIB needed to be controlled and was therefore also subject to the requirements of the L28 Approved Code of Practice (2nd ed) for the Control of Asbestos at Work Regulations 1987.

The regulations require employers doing work on these three materials (asbestos insulation, asbestos coatings and asbestos insulating board) to hold a valid licence from the HSE. Part of the licence condition is that work will be notified to the relevant enforcing authority.

There are two main exemptions to the requirement to hold a licence:

(a) The first is where the amount of work to be done is small – less than two hours in total in any seven-day period and not more than one hour per person. The "work" time includes the preparation and clean-up as well as time spent working on the asbestos. It would not necessarily include other time spent on ancillary repairs, for example, where asbestos is not being disturbed. Even though a licence is not required, CAWR 2002 (and the ACoP L27) still applies.

(b) The second exemption is where an employer uses his own staff to do work on his own premises, which the employer occupies.

In this case, however, the employer must also notify the appropriate enforcing authority of his intention to do this work and clearly must do the work in accordance with the CAWR 2002.

The other exemptions would be for air sampling and bulk sampling as part of a survey. It would clearly not be required for work on bonded materials such as asbestos cement, asbestos floor tiles or asbestos roofing felt. Textured coatings (such as "Artex"), however, are included as they are deemed to be a coating containing asbestos. Sealing AIB in poor condition would also require a licence.

There are a number of additional activities which require a licence under these regulations:

(a) Supervision of a contractor doing asbestos removal work.
    There are now many consultancies who hold a "Supervisory Licence". They are not allowed to do the removal work themselves but they will need to submit a notification to the enforcing authority together with a suitable plan of work covering their work. HSE will expect supervising consultants to have at least the same level of training and qualification as for any other asbestos removal contractor's supervisor.
(b) Erection and dismantling of scaffold platforms for asbestos removal
    If it is reasonably foreseeable that the asbestos may be disturbed during the scaffold erection, the scaffold contractor is required to hold an ancillary licence, but again, he is not allowed to do the asbestos work unless he also holds a full removal licence.
(c) Testing and maintaining vacuum cleaners and negative pressure units used for asbestos removal.
    If the employer only operates at his own premises, the exemption for the employer on his own premises applies (see above).

A licence is issued in the first place for one year, but only after the licensing inspector has thoroughly examined the applicant's records, procedures and experience. The licence is then reviewed by the HSE after the first year and if the employer's performance is deemed to be satisfactory, the licence will be renewed for a three-year period (but no longer). Each renewal thereafter will require the licence-holder's work and records to be thoroughly checked by the HSE. This is by no means a simple formality. At present, HSE inspectors are likely to make site visits to contractors whose licence is due for renewal in the next six months.

Where an employer (contractor) is carrying out work which disturbs asbestos, it is the licence holder's responsibility to notify the work to the appropriate enforcing authority 14 days before the work begins. The notification is on a form known as ASB5 and must be accompanied by the employer's plan of work. HSE will take a very dim view of work starting before the full 14 day notification is completed and are likely to issue a prohibition notice. The employer must not assume, however, that, even though the HSE have seen the plan of work, they have approved it.

## CDM Regulations 1994

The construction industry – together with agriculture – has for many years had one of the worst safety records with unacceptable fatality rates on construction sites. The objective of the CDM regulations was to try to provide a better structure for the management of health and safety on site. Where demolition is taking place and asbestos is known or suspected to be present, the planning supervisor is required to ensure that a Type 3 survey (see chapter 6) has been carried out and is included in the pre-tender health and safety plan which is handed over to the principal contractor for the construction phase. The asbestos removal must, of course, be completed before the demolition is allowed to continue.

On the conclusion of the asbestos works, the Health and Safety File (to be returned to the client) needs to contain reference to or records of:

- certificates for re-occupation after asbestos removal
- consignment notes of asbestos waste disposal
- records of asbestos remaining in the site
- amendments needed to the asbestos register for the site

## Special Waste Regulations 1996

All the materials to be discussed here are classified as a special waste. The definition of a special waste (as far as asbestos is concerned) is a material containing more than 0.1% asbestos (of any type or mixture) by weight. Asbestos is one of the exceptions in that waste asbestos generated by a private householder from his domestic premises is still a special waste and must be disposed of correctly.

The requirements of the regulations are that the material should be disposed of as a hazardous waste to a registered landfill site. The purpose of the disposal is so that adequate records can be kept and to prevent future disturbance or dispersal of the waste.

Transfer to the waste site must be by a registered carrier with a consignment note. The transfer must be notified to the Environment Agency at least 72 hours before the transfer begins.

Disposal of the waste is subject to a landfill tax and because of this, most local authorities have reported a significant increase in "fly-tipping" of asbestos waste since the regulations were introduced. The cost of disposal is likely to increase because of new regulations in 2004 which will restrict the number of landfill sites where asbestos can be disposed of.

# RIDDOR (Reporting of Injuries, Diseases and Dangerous Occurrences Regulations 1995)

RIDDOR is primarily for the gathering of information by the HSE, for example so that they can prioritise their work. The major asbestos diseases are notified to HSE through the death certificates, which must include the primary cause of death and possibly other contributory factors.

However, the reporting requirement also covers "dangerous occurrences" which the guidance makes clear should include:

(a) Uncontrolled disturbance of asbestos materials (eg an electrician drilling holes through asbestos insulating board).
(b) Accidental escape of asbestos dust from an enclosure into an occupied area.

Not only should the people exposed be notified but also the incident needs to be reported to the HSE.

# MHSAW 1999

The HSE regard the MHSAW Regulations as second in importance only to the HSWA 1974 itself. It actually says nothing specific about asbestos but the requirement is to assess (and manage) all risks in a workplace and this is deemed to include asbestos.

At the time of the introduction of CAWR 2002, there was quite an internal debate within HSE as to whether the new regulation was needed. The argument was that the Management Regulations required an employer to make an adequate assessment of all risks at work and to manage those risks. (It would be difficult to do an "adequate assessment" of risks from asbestos if the employer did not have reliable information about the asbestos in the premises!) Eventually HSE decided the "duty to manage" needed to be made explicit within the Control of Asbestos at Work Regulations.

The MHSAW Regulations allow an employer to bring in outside expertise to assist in the management of a specific hazard, provided adequate information is provided to the consultant. The regulations, however, also now make it clear that the employer should give preference to internal resources and therefore consider suitable training for their own employee.

# Asbestos (Prohibitions) Regulations 1992 (amended 1999)

Asbestos materials have gradually been phased out of use over a 30-year period from 1969 to 1999. The first step was the trade ban on the used of crocidolite in 1969. This coincided with the clear establishment of the link with mesothelioma and the recognition that the health effects of asbestos could not be ignored any longer. Crocidolite was recognised as the most dangerous type of asbestos and industry did not import any more after 1969 although stocks undoubtedly continued to be used for several years. Amosite was imported until the mid 1970s and finished goods containing amosite were imported right up to the eventual prohibition of the import, supply, manufacture of materials. The import and use of amosite slowed greatly by 1980, but both crocidolite and amosite were finally prohibited only in 1985, with the first Asbestos (Prohibitions) Regulations 1985.

The legal prohibition in 1985 covered the import, supply and manufacture of materials containing amosite and crocidolite, and the installations of these materials.

A new set of regulations in 1992 had the effect of extending the prohibition on the import, processing, supply and use to include all the minor asbestos types (anthophyllite, tremolite and actinolite) – so that now all the amphibole asbestos minerals were prohibited. At this stage, only certain low risk chrysotile materials were still allowed to be produced, such as asbestos cement, roofing felt (until the end of 1992) and friction products. Textiles could only be used if sealed to prevent fibre release.

Finally, after a confrontation with the Canadian Government in 1997, the import and application of all asbestos was prohibited with the Asbestos (Prohibitions) (Amendments) Regulations 1999. A number of temporary exemptions were allowed for applications where a suitable non-asbestos substitute had not yet been developed. To all intents and purposes, all forms of asbestos can no longer be used in the UK. However, surveyors may still find stocks of gasket materials, rope or cement sheet – ready to be used by those who are not aware of what the material is or do not realise it is prohibited.

# Training for Asbestos Surveyors

## Introduction

The HSE regards training – "information, instruction, training and supervision" – as of paramount importance. Its significance stretches back right through to the HSWA 1974 from section 2(2)(b). This has been emphasized recently with the proposed publication of the Licensed Contractors Guide and the Analysts Guide, both of which place great stress on training, for operatives and supervisors doing asbestos removal work and on analysts doing surveys and clearance inspections after removal. Absence of formal qualifications as an asbestos surveyor may be regarded as an offence under regulation 9 of CAWR 2002.

Regulation 9 (1) (b)

> Every employer shall ensure that adequate information, instruction and training is given to those of his employees ... who carry out work in connection with the employer's duties, so that they can carry out that work effectively.

In other words, a surveyor who cannot demonstrate adequate training and qualification is at risk of falling foul of the regulations, although this regulation would only be invoked where an incompetent survey had come to the notice of the enforcing authorities.

For the purposes of health and safety, of course, a self-employed person is treated as both an employer and an employee.

For many years, the HSE have been increasingly concerned at the standard of training and competence of analysts out in the field – and also of contractors and their operatives. For the analysts, the HSE have therefore been instrumental in establishing better training schemes and qualifications and ensuring that UKAS insists on these qualifications for analysts and surveyors where the organisations are accredited by UKAS.

The recognised training schemes and qualifications for the industry are almost exclusively provided by the British Occupational Hygiene Society (BOHS) and its academic and professional branch, the Faculty of Occupational Hygiene (FOH). The FOH has a number of levels of academic and professional qualifications and it must be remembered that its principal interest is the field of occupational hygiene, which covers a multitude of workplace hazards such as toxic chemicals and physical matters such as noise and vibration, ergonomics and non-ionising radiation. Asbestos is just a small part of the field of interest of the Society but is very large in terms of activity for the FOH – perhaps occupying about 90% of its time.

The qualifications range from the Diploma in Occupational Hygiene (Dip Occ Hyg) down to the Proficiency Modules in Asbestos. The Proficiency Modules were developed at the request (and with input from) the HSE. HSE have now insisted that UKAS include these as evidence of training in training records.

The full range of modules at the basic level include:

P401    Identification of asbestos in bulk samples (PLM).
P402    Building surveys and bulk sampling for asbestos (including risk assessment and risk management strategies).
P403    Asbestos fibre counting (PCM).
P404    Air sampling and clearance testing of asbestos.
P405    Management of asbestos in buildings (safe removal and disposal).

These modules are not exclusively aimed at asbestos analysts (but they are obviously the main target audience) and indeed analysts need other training courses as well, for example, on general health and safety.

The intention of these modules is to provide basic training in the techniques and practice of the subject material. It is important to realise that they do not necessarily demonstrate "competence" as such, rather a limited demonstration of initial basic training and achievement of some degree of capability in the technique. True proficiency will only come with the extended experience in the laboratory or in the field – and that can only be gained with weeks or months of work which will need to be supervised or reviewed by senior staff.

A better name for these courses would have been "Preliminary Modules" to indicate their introductory nature. Unfortunately, BOHS already had a set of Preliminary Certificates in Occupational Hygiene, which are substantial week-long courses (originally two weeks!). They were therefore understandably reluctant to name these courses Preliminary Modules because they were seen as a lower level qualification than the Preliminary Certificates as they lasted only two or three days each. BOHS were anxious to protect the professional status of the Preliminary Certificates or Modules because they contributed to the award of their overall Certificate of Competence in Occupational Hygiene (Cert Occ Hyg).

The name "Proficiency Module" has, however, given rise to the very unfortunate impression that someone having passed a Proficiency Module is "competent" in that area – and that is by no means necessarily the case. Without good field or laboratory experience – several weeks or months, in most cases – the operator cannot be regarded as "competent".

# BOHS P402 Proficiency Module

P402 now is the standard qualification in asbestos sampling and surveying. Several thousand candidates have passed through this qualification route, although other qualifications are in the process of being developed through National Individual Asbestos Certification Scheme (NIACS), for example, through the Royal Institute of Chartered Surveyors (RICS).

P402 is a three day course, covering the basic legislative requirements (CAWR regulation 4, MHSAW 1999, etc), the occurrence and technical properties of asbestos, the usages to which they have been put, sampling techniques and the conduct of surveys, assessment of materials and priority assessments.

The examination consists of two parts, a multiple choice question paper set and marked by BOHS, and practical assessments, either by the course provider/tutor or by an independent external assessor. The assessments cover a number of practical matters, including:

- recognition of materials (both asbestos and non-asbestos) from sealed samples and/or in pictures or video presentations
- knowledge of building terms and construction techniques
- the ability to sample materials safely (especially pipe insulation as core samples) and the use of appropriate Personal Protective Equipment (PPE) and RPE
- the ability to carry out the materials risk assessments and priority assessments (as in MDHS 100 and HSG 227)
- the ability to provide suitable recommendations for remedial works.

The assessor is usually the course provider. They have to be approved by BOHS, and this means that they must hold (at least) the S301 qualification with the oral examination as a "Competent Person". The assessor cannot assess any candidates who are connected with their own organisation, so although consultancies can run P402 as an internal course for their staff, they must bring in an external independent assessor for the practical assessment. There is indeed a suggestion that all courses should be assessed independently.

This is evidently a difficult area, to ensure that assessments are equally, correctly and fairly applied. BOHS have therefore introduced a quality control function to audit assessments provided at courses, so that assessors are reviewed to ensure that assessments are being conducted to the correct standard.

## Evidence of field proficiency

The course provides very little time to be able to do "real" surveys. This is not a problem when candidates already have some experience of field survey work, but for new surveyors, this can make the course rather theoretical without any chance to apply the theory in practice. They may be able to pass the written exam and the assessments but they hardly make a "competent" surveyor. Three days in a classroom does not make a fully-fledged asbestos surveyor.

BOHS recognise this, of course, and in order to complete the module, candidates have six months in which to supply BOHS with copies of two surveys which they have done for review by BOHS. The surveys must be either Type 2 or Type 3 (ie include some sampling) and must be the entire work of the candidate, albeit under the supervision of a senior surveyor. It is not acceptable for two or more surveyors from the same organisation to submit reports of the same building. BOHS will (and do) check for this.

These survey reports are scrutinised carefully. In the early days, about 20–25% of reports were being rejected as unsuitable, for a wide variety of reasons. In some cases, for example, the analytical reports did not agree with the samples recorded in the report.

# BOHS S301 Specialist Module

The BOHS Specialist Module S301 – "Asbestos and other fibres" – was the original course on asbestos. In the absence of anything else, this was accepted as the standard professional qualification in asbestos consultancy. It is a week-long course which, as the title implies, covers aspects of other industrial fibres such as man-made vitreous fibres (fibre glass, rock wool, mineral wools, refractory ceramic fibres) and organic fibres such as aramids (eg "Kevlar"). The one additional area covered here is health effects of asbestos and other fibres: these are specifically not covered anywhere in the Proficiency Modules, although some course providers do refer to them.

S301 covers all the topics covered by the Proficiency Modules, but since the course duration is only a week (compared to two or three days for each of the Proficiency Modules) there is no time to gain "proficiency" in the analytical techniques. The theory is covered but proficiency can only be gained later. The original intention was that this module was appropriate for practitioners with about six months practical and analytical experience.

Since the examination includes a brief written essay, candidates have to demonstrate a degree of fluency and accuracy in writing and the ability to apply the information acquired. A good educational background – for example, at least to "A" Level standard or first degree level – is therefore highly desirable, although by no means essential. Attendance at the course is not essential; many candidates with good experience are able to pass the examination without sitting the full course.

The S301 qualification clearly does not confer "competence" in asbestos consultancy activities, and especially in the analytical techniques. This qualification is therefore supplemented by an oral examination to assess experience and competence. The BOHS rules state that a candidate for the oral examination must have a minimum of six months field experience and they must submit a piece of written work to be assessed. This can be in the form of a survey report, a clearance report or any other material which demonstrates some significant activity other than just some analysis of bulk samples or fibre counting.

The oral examination is usually in front of a panel of three examiners, (who are themselves being reviewed to ensure the examination is fair). The candidate may be questioned on their written work (particularly if there are queries on the technical content) but must also be able to demonstrate experience and proficiency in all areas. If there are any significant gaps in their experience and capability, they will automatically fail. This is a tough examination and BOHS expect candidates to have a thorough grasp of the subject and – most importantly – to be able to express information and arguments lucidly, accurately and fluently. Above all, they need to be able to demonstrate a "professional" approach to the subject. They should be up to date with legislation and guidance from HSE, with knowledge of the health effects and possess a good understanding of the meaning of control limits and action levels.

The oral examination is optional, but the written examination on its own does not carry very much weight, with BOHS, UKAS or HSE. UKAS requires that at least one person in the accredited organisation must hold the qualification of S301 with the oral examination as a Competent Person, or a higher or equivalent qualification.

## Other qualifications

UKAS accepts other BOHS qualifications which are of a higher standard, including:

- Certificate of Operational Competence in Occupational Hygiene (Cert Occ Hyg)
- Diploma of Professional Competence on Occupational Hygiene (Dip Occ Hyg)

Both of these qualifications cover the much broader field of occupational hygiene. They include a study of asbestos within the course content, but it may be arguable whether it includes the level of practical experience in surveys that would be required. (See also chapter 3 on Accreditation.)

# Site experience

It has been emphasized in all the discussion above that site or field experience is essential. The use of two-person teams for surveying premises for asbestos is invaluable for training new surveyors. It assumes, of course, that a competent experienced surveyor who is also a good trainer is training the new surveyor.

The trainee's training record needs to show:

- which surveys he/she has been on, including type of premises and survey type
- what activities undertaken (eg sampling)
- the number of days on site
- any assessment of performance by the supervising surveyor.

The trainee needs to see a variety of premises. Training in surveys of domestic properties does not equip a surveyor to inspect a chemical plant or a power station, for example. As a rough guide, surveyors should have experience of the following-

- domestic premises
- office-type locations
- retail premises
- education and health-care premises
- heavy engineering and chemical industrial sites
- demolition sites (for Type 3 surveys) which will cover all of the above.

# Audits

As an on-going check of survey performance, individual surveyors should be audited as part of an in-house quality assurance programme at least once a year. This would certainly be a requirement under EN 45004 or ISO 17020. It should pick up surveyors who are either developing bad habits or not working in compliance with current procedures and guidance. This audit should cover all aspects of the survey, including:

- survey preparation, paperwork and instructions
- safety risk assessments
- survey equipment (including PPE and RPE)
- survey conduct and procedures, including access to all areas reasonably accessible, and recognition of all asbestos containing materials
- sampling techniques
- documentation and risk assessments
- remedial works and recommendations
- preparation of the final report or register.

The results of any such audit should be recorded. Non-compliances or errors will need to be dealt with in the quality management system.

# Refresher training

This will be discussed again under chapter 13, but it is worth remembering that CAWR 2002 requires that all persons working with asbestos should receive appropriate training "at regular intervals", ie refresher training. The ACoP L27 ("Work which does not normally require a licence") and L28 ("Work with asbestos coatings, asbestos insulation and asbestos insulating board") both make it clear that the refresher training should be at least annually or when methods or procedures change. The requirement for refresher training applies to asbestos surveyors and analysts as much as to asbestos removal operatives.

Refresher training attempts to deal with two problems. First, people (surveyors as well as removal operatives) can get blasé about the risks and forget their training or develop bad habits. Second, however, standards and procedures develop and regulations change. It is therefore necessary to ensure that people are fully up to date with "best practice" – techniques and procedures – in the field.

It is fair to say that asbestos as a safety matter is one of the most heavily regulated areas, but also one with the most rapid changes in standards and procedures.

# Accreditation

## Legal requirements for accreditation

The HSE are fully convinced of the benefits of accreditation. It should be remembered that much of the asbestos consultancy business has grown out of areas which have not had a solid technical, academic or professional background. Historically, asbestos removal operations (including air sampling, analysis and surveying) have suffered from poor standards and the HSE have been fighting a continual battle to improve techniques and standards over the last two decades and more.

With the absence of a sound professional basis in many laboratories, it is clearly important to insist on a structured quality management system, covering the management of people, equipment and methods in such a way as to ensure that high quality standards are achieved. This is now available for asbestos sampling and testing with ISO/IEC 17025 (which superseded BS EN 45001).

The legal requirements for accreditation have been introduced in a series of steps, beginning with the Control of Asbestos at Work (Amendment) Regulations 1992. The ACoP L28 (2nd ed) ("Work with asbestos coatings, asbestos insulation and asbestos insulating board") required laboratories carrying out air sampling and fibre counting to be accredited for both activities – previously nearly all (if not all) laboratories would have been accredited only for fibre counting.

With the Control of Asbestos at Work (Amendment) Regulations 1998, the regulations finally made it a statutory requirement for laboratories offering these services to be accredited. The exemption was for an employer's laboratory which only needed to have a quality system which complied with the relevant sections of BS EN 45001, and not necessarily to be accredited by United Kingdom Accreditation Service (UKAS). (An example of this would have been a laboratory in a power station carrying out air monitoring on the station premises for their own information.)

There are no statutory requirements for accreditation for surveying at the time of writing. When the CAWR 2002 were proposed, the possibility of accreditation by UKAS had still not been introduced. The problem UKAS faced was that surveying of buildings for asbestos requires the surveyor to "inspect", to use his professional knowledge and experience and not simply to "measure" or "calibrate" using a standard method for which ISO/IEC 17025 would be appropriate.

UKAS therefore had to develop accreditation to BS EN 45004 for inspection of buildings for asbestos and run a pilot programme for about 40 organisations. This was completed in October 2002 and now about 80 organisations are accredited.

It is very likely that when the CAWR 2002 Regulations are amended, perhaps in 2005 or 2006, the HSE will take the opportunity to introduce a requirement for either accreditation to BS EN 45004 (ISO/IEC 17020) or individual certification to BS EN 45013 (to be replaced by ISO/IEC 17024 in April 2005).

## UKAS

UKAS is the sole accreditation body in the UK. It began life within the DTI (Department of Trade and Industry) as NAMAS, which itself was an amalgamation of the British Calibration Service (BCS) and the National Testing Laboratory Accreditation Scheme (NATLAS). It is now a privatised body and self funded. Because of the privatisation (and essentially a monopoly) UKAS and its fees have been heavily criticised over the years, but there is no doubt it has an important role to play and HSE sees UKAS as a critical part of the way to achieve quality.

A laboratory or organisation seeking accreditation will be assigned to an assessment manager within UKAS. The assessment manager will be assisted by a technical assessor, not usually an employee of UKAS, but a technical expert within the field. It may sometimes be the case that a laboratory does not feel able to accept a technical assessor because he/she is perceived as a competitor within the field. UKAS will try to accommodate this factor but obviously within a tightly knit area, there are bound sometimes to be conflicts.

The accreditation process begins with the application to UKAS by the laboratory/organisation for accreditation. The application must be accompanied by the quality manual, describing how the organisation is structured and detailing how it fulfils the requirements of the quality standard. UKAS will review the quality manual and decide whether it appears to meet the standard and, if so, will then probably arrange a pre-assessment meeting to discuss the procedures and workings of the organisation's systems.

Once this is agreed, there will be a formal assessment visit to the laboratory to observe the activities being accredited, examine the systems and associated documentation. In the case of site activities such as surveying, the assessment will include visits to see surveys in operation. Any non-conformities found by the assessors will have to be discharged before accreditation is granted.

Assessment visits are usually made by the assessment manager and the technical assessor together. The assessment duties are usually split between them but the presence of the assessment manager is to ensure that the assessment is applied fairly and that the system is consistent with the accreditation standard.

After accreditation is granted, a follow-up surveillance visit by UKAS takes place within six months to confirm that the systems are functioning and surveillance visits then take place annually. Re-assessment of the laboratory will take place after three years. Technical assessors will be usually replaced at the reassessment to ensure that the laboratory is seen by a variety of assessors and to make the application of the standard consistent across all laboratories.

## ISO/IEC 17020 (BS EN 45004)

In addition to the standard itself, there are two crucial UKAS documents for accreditation of inspection bodies:

1.  EA-5/01 Guidance on the Application of BS EN 45004 (ISO/IEC 17020)
    This was written by the inspection committee of the body referred to as European Co-operation for Accreditation, in order

to achieve harmonised implementation of inspection body accreditation within Europe.

2. RG8 Accreditation of Bodies Surveying for Asbestos in Premises
   This is the UKAS guidance for the accreditation of inspection bodies to BS EN 45004 (ISO/IEC 17020).

Both of these documents can be downloaded from the UKAS web site http://www.ukas.org. The standards themselves (ISO/IEC versions) are obtainable from the ISO web site http://www.iso.org.

BS EN 45004 and ISO/IEC 17020 are exactly equivalent. The application of ISO/IEC 17020 to surveying for asbestos in buildings is described in the UKAS document RG8. RG8 makes it clear that inspection body accreditation should not be confused with personnel certification – which is for individuals by a certification body (see below). ISO/IEC 17020 imposes certain additional requirements on the quality system of the inspection body which will include audits of its inspectors or surveyors.

One area specifically addressed is the "independence, impartiality and integrity" of the surveying organisation. A conflict of interest could arise if the surveying organisation has connections or involvement in further work, such as remedial works, removal or consultancy. The standard therefore describes inspection bodies as Type A, B or C, depending on their relationship to, or independence from, the client.

Type A bodies are third party, independent of the client and other parties involved.

Type B bodies are part (distinct and separate) of a parent organisation and supply services only to that body.

Type C bodies are those which may be part of a larger organisation but which also offer inspection services to external clients as well as their own organisation. Where other staff may be involved in activities such as removal or consultancy, the organisation must demonstrate "safeguards" to ensure adequate segregation of responsibilities and accountabilities.

In practice, most asbestos consultancies will be classified as a Type C body because they will be associated with other activities which may be perceived as a potential conflict of interest. RG8 makes it clear that a Type C body must not offer (or be offered) any inducement (eg fee discount) if they gain from any subsequent associated works, repairs or removal.

An organisation may be accredited for surveys, even though it sub-contracts the sampling and/or the analysis of the samples. Where it sub-contracts sampling, this must be to an organisation accredited by UKAS for the collection of asbestos samples (see UKAS LAB 30 document) and analysis should also be carried out (if sub-contracted) by a laboratory accredited for the analysis or which can demonstrate an equivalent level of competence. (Note that, however, analytical laboratories offering this service will have to be accredited from 21 November 2004).

Organisations may be accredited for any or all of the survey types (Type 1, 2 or 3) as defined in MDHS 100, including the materials risk assessment for Types 1 and 2. An organisation can also be accredited for the management priority assessment as in HSG 227.

# Quality management system

RG8 as an implementation of ISO/IEC 17020 requires a number of specific items.

## *Training and experience*

The requirements are documented in UKAS document RG8, para 8. A qualified surveyor must have P402 (or equivalent or higher qualification) plus field experience plus on-site witnessing of performance during a minimum number of surveys by a technically competent assessor.

| Survey type | Minimum qualification | Minimum experience | Knowledge |
|---|---|---|---|
| 1 | P402 or higher/ equivalent | Six months appropriate site experience | Range, location and uses of asbestos products; types and ages of premises |
| | | plus | |
| | | Five surveys witnessed and assessed | Homogeneity of products, sampling strategies, health and safety implications Current regulations, codes of practice and guidance |
| 2 | (As for Type 1) | Six months appropriate site experience | (As for Type 1) |

| Survey type | Minimum qualification | Minimum experience | Knowledge |
|---|---|---|---|
| 3 | (As for Type 1) | plus Five Type 2 surveys witnessed and assessed Six months appropriate site experience plus Five Type 2 or 3 surveys (minimum 2 Type 3) witnessed and assessed | (As for Type 1) |

The surveyors must be witnessed and assessed by a technically competent person (ie someone who is a fully qualified surveyor). Individual records need to show the experience and ability to survey in a range of types of premises (domestic, industrial, commercial) to demonstrate adequate experience in those premises.

## Inspection procedures

The inspection procedures must be documented. MDHS 100 (Surveying, sampling and assessment of asbestos containing materials) provides a basic framework but the inspection body needs to develop its own procedures, instructions and checklists. The checks will include a contract review to ensure that the client's instructions are being met. It must also include assessments of safety hazards which may be encountered on site with appropriate control measures to protect staff and any others who may be affected by the work.

Equipment needed includes the survey sampling equipment, access equipment and materials needed to make good sampling points where necessary.

RG8 requires that individual surveyors be audited while carrying out surveys on site at least once per year to ensure that they maintain the standards required by the accreditation standard. The on-site witnessing of surveys must be done by a technically competent person who is sufficiently independent to able to assess the surveyor with objectivity.

MDHS 100 also requires that a proportion of surveys should be subject to quality assurance checks and these are normally carried out on site at the same time as the survey and as the audit of the surveyors.

# Individual certification (BS EN 45013 or ISO/IEC 17024)

The cost of accreditation is such that accreditation for surveyors to ISO/IEC 17020 is appropriate only for larger organisations, with, say 20 surveyors or more. For smaller organisations, say partnerships of four or five surveyors, certification to BS EN 45013 or ISO/IEC 17024 will be more realistic. For ISO/IEC 17020, effectively the inspection body certifies its surveyors. For BS EN 45013, the surveyors are certified by another independent certifying body. In the case of ISO/IEC 17020, the inspection body, however, also provides a management structure, which is not necessarily present under BS EN 45013. This is a matter of some concern, since HSE are concerned that the two standards should provide similar quality output.

There are currently two certification schemes, either in operation or in development, ABICS (Asbestos Buildings Inspectors Certification Scheme) and NIACS (National Individual Asbestos Certification Scheme).

## *ABICS*

ABICS is operated by BOHS and was launched in April 2004 and will be accredited by UKAS. It presumes a surveyor to have a P402 qualification but also requires them to demonstrate a level of knowledge and experience at a panel interview.

For ABICS, the only qualification accepted is the P402 exam and assessment together with the required surveys to demonstrate field proficiency. Interestingly, ABICS will not accept the alternative BOHS qualifications permitted by UKAS in RG8 (S301 plus oral as "competent person in asbestos", Cert Occ Hyg or Dip Occ Hyg), regarding the specific knowledge gained in P402 as indispensable.

As well as the qualification, surveyors must be able to demonstrate at least six months field experience in a range of asbestos survey types and submit reports for assessment. They will then be required to attend a formal interview which will include an assessment of their sampling techniques.

To maintain their certification they will need to carry out at least a minimum level of work and submit annually a log of surveys they have done. ABICS will then select at random surveys, copies of which must be submitted to ABICS for review.

## *NIACS*

NIACS is run by a partnership originally set up between ARCA (Asbestos Removal Contractors Association) and RICS (Royal Institute of Chartered Surveyors). It was intended to be open mainly for members of the Institute, and RICS at the start expected its surveyors to do Type 1 inspections only – and to sub-contract any sampling needed.

Its certified surveyors are required to attend a five-day course which will lead to a qualification to undertake Type 1 surveys. Holders of the BOHS P402 qualification will gain only partial exemption for this course. To complete the qualification and to progress to qualification for Types 2 and 3 surveys, they will need to submit a summary of their surveys and examples for assessment, together with a formal interview. This is very similar to the requirements set by ABICS.

This qualification will enable surveyors to get professional indemnity cover for their asbestos survey work through RICS, and the certifying bodies will certainly require that their certificated surveyors carry adequate amounts of PI cover.

# Asbestos Sources and Properties

## Mineral types

As defined in the current regulations, asbestos is a collection of naturally occurring crystalline fibrous silicate minerals. The formation of these would mostly have been through a metamorphic process, ie rocks subjected to conditions of heat and pressure to produce the fibrous crystalline form, but geologists are not at all clear as to the precise mechanisms that lead to the mineral formations. Asbestos minerals generally appear in veins up to, say, 10 to 15 cm in thickness, with the fibres running perpendicular to the vein.

There are two main types of asbestos, *amphibole* and *serpentine*, which are quite distinct with different physical and chemical properties; these properties ultimately determine the useful commercial applications as well as their well-established harmful effects. The amphiboles are members of a group known as chain silicates, whereas serpentine chrysotile is a sheet or a layer silicate.

The amphiboles are, in some cases, related and represent variations in chemical composition from the original material, particularly in the magnesium:iron ratio. They are based on the silicate tetrahedral structures, referred to as chain silicates, with additional metal ions and hydroxyl groups. Of the amphibole minerals, five exist in the fibrous or asbestiform habit. Fibrous serpentine is known as chrysotile, and is the only fibrous member of the group.

**Table 4.1** Compositions of the asbestos minerals

| Serpentine | Formula | Non-fibrous forms | Colour |
|---|---|---|---|
| Chrysotile | $Mg_3Si_2O_5(OH)_4$ | Lizardite, antigorite | White |
| | | | |
| Amphibole | Formula | Non-fibrous forms | Colour |
| Amosite | $(Mg,Fe^{2+})_7Si_8O_{22}(OH)_2$ | Grunerite | Brown |
| Crocidolite | $Na_2Fe^{2+}_3Fe^{3+}_2Si_8O_{22}(OH)_2$ | Riebeckite | Blue |
| Anthophyllite | $(Mg,Fe^{2+})_7Si_8O_{22}(OH,F)_2$ | | Beige to Off-white |
| Tremolite | $Ca_2(Mg,Fe^{2+})_5Si_8O_{22}(OH,F)_2$ | | White |
| Actinolite | $Ca_2(Mg,Fe^{2+})_5Si_8O_{22}(OH,F)_2$ | | Green |

Deer, Howie and Zussman, *An Introduction to the Rock-Forming Minerals* 2nd ed, 1992. pp 223–275

The chemical formulae quoted above represent average compositions from a number of sources, and, as indicated, the precise Mg:Fe ratios in some of the amphiboles may vary from one source to another, but may equally be described as the particular mineral in question.

There are no differently named forms of the non-fibrous versions of the three less common asbestos minerals. The fibrous asbestiform minerals should now be referred to as anthophyllite asbestos, tremolite asbestos and actinolite asbestos.

Amosite is sometimes referred to as montasite, but this is a magnesium-rich composition and softer than the harsher iron-rich amosite. In the UK only the name amosite is used for this mineral. The name "amosite" derives from its principal commercial source South Africa – "Asbestos Mines Of South Africa". It is also referred to in some of the waste classifications as mysorite.

Tremolite and actinolite are related in a series of minerals (tremolite – ferro-actinolite), the identity of each depending on the iron content, where iron or magnesium occupy cation sites in the crystal lattice. The highest iron content of the series is in ferro-actinolite but this does not appear to exist in an asbestiform habit. Tremolite and actinolite exist in a solid-solution series so that in some cases it may be difficult to distinguish categorically between the two minerals. The refractive index measurement used in identification of the minerals by polarised light microscopy is usually quite distinct, but where they exist, they may be referred to as "tremolite-actinolite". In practice, where the minerals are used in commercial applications, it usually appears as tremolite; actinolite (although a regulated fibre) is hardly known to have been used commercially.

The amphibole fibres appear very straight, harsh, elastic (springy), whereas chrysotile fibres are much softer, silky and inelastic. The serpentine chrysotile is classified as a sheet or a layer silicate, but its structure is a double layer, with a brucite (magnesium hydroxide) layer parallel to the silicate tetrahedra layer. Because the inter-atomic spacing of the magnesium hydroxide is wider than the silicate tetrahedra, it forces the sheet to deform into curved layers – the chrysotile fibrils therefore appear either as concentric cylinders (Yada K, 1971, *Acta Cryst*, **A27**, pp 659–64) or as a scroll-type structure (Deer, Howie and Zussman, *op cit* p 347).

It should be noted that chrysotile is not infrequently found with low levels of tremolite, perhaps up to about 1%, although other sources in the literature report even higher levels. The asbestos textile industry in the UK at one stage was screening raw chrysotile asbestos for the presence of tremolite, because it was appreciated that tremolite as an amphibole would have more significant health effects.

Tremolite is also found in other minerals, such as olivine, also a magnesium silicate. Olivine is very hard and is used for grit blasting in the UK, and so has recently been the subject of scrutiny for airborne asbestos fibres in dry grit blasting operations. Tremolite is also found in talc and, of course, cosmetic talc is screened for the absence of tremolite.

Tremolite and actinolite are also found in some deposits of vermiculite, and recent reports of asbestos-related diseases around the Libby mine in Montana have caused concern in the area. The Libby mine vermiculite was sold under the trade name of "Zonolite". Vermiculite imported into the UK mostly came from South Africa but this was screened for the absence of tremolite-actinolite. Vermiculite was used for a range of materials, such as loft insulation, and cavity wall insulation, as well as a light-weight board ("Vicuclad"), spray coatings ("Mandolite" or "Fendolite") and is still used as a soil-less compost or horticultural product.

# Sources and recent production trends

Of the six regulated asbestos minerals, chrysotile – the only fibrous serpentine – is by far the most common and constitutes about 90–95% of all the asbestos which has been mined and used in industrial applications. It is a ubiquitous, abundant mineral, found throughout the world. Deposits can even be found in the UK, but have not been mined commercially. The other amphiboles are much less common.

The major producers of chrysotile have always been Canada and Russia. The Canadian mines started in the late 1870s and were the principal producers up to 1970. Although the Russian mines appear to have been opened in the early 1800s (before the Canadian mines) production did not overtake Canada until the latter started to decline in the 1970s.

Over the 20th century, chrysotile asbestos has been produced from every continent. In 1950, there were records of commercial asbestos production in 29 countries around the world.

Total world production between 1900 and 2000 is estimated to have been 173 million tons.

**Fig. 4.1** World production 1920–2000 for the main centres

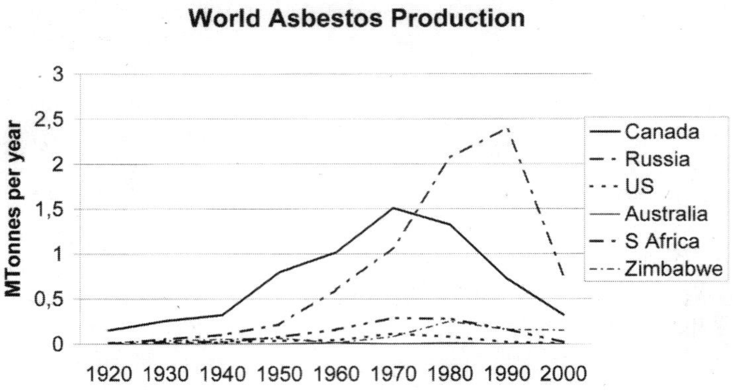

Robert L Virta, US Geological Survey, World-wide Asbestos Supply and Trends from 1900 to 2000, Report 03-83

In contrast, the amphiboles have been derived from much fewer sources in smaller quantities. The main producer of crocidolite has always been South Africa, where it is reported production began as early as 1893, peaked in 1977 at about 201,000 tons and continued until about 1997. Amosite production began in South Africa in 1907, peaking at 106,000 tons, but ceasing production in 1992. Crocidolite was also produced in Western Australia but ceased in 1983. It was also produced in very small quantities – a few hundred tons per year – mostly, if not entirely, for domestic use in Bolivia.

The general realisation of the adverse health effects of the amphibole asbestos minerals led to a sharp drop in demand for both amosite and crocidolite from about 1970.

Anthophyllite was mainly produced in Finland from about 1919 to 1975. Indeed, the presence of anthophyllite has been found in Finnish pottery dated to about 2,500 BC, one of the earliest known occurrences of asbestos in man-made materials. North Carolina was a producer of anthophyllite in the US and other sources were from Mozambique and India. Tremolite was mainly from Italy, US (California) and India.

**Fig 4.2** Use of asbestos in UK and other European countries; 1920–2000

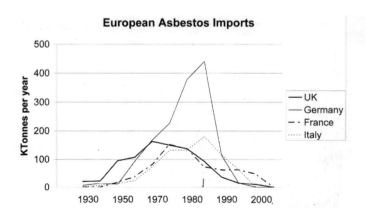

Robert L Virta, US Geological Survey, World-wide Asbestos Supply and Trends from 1900 to 2000, Report 03-83

As seen in Fig. 4.2, the United Kingdom was the earliest large-scale user of asbestos in Western Europe, later followed (and overtaken) by Germany and France. Clearly, the old British Empire trade connections with Canada, South Africa, Australia and Zimbabwe (formerly Rhodesia) have been very important and have led to the UK being a major manufacturing centre and consumer of asbestos products.

**Fig 4.3** An abandoned chrysotile open-cast mine in the Troodos Mountains, Cyprus

# The chemical and physical properties of the minerals

The main physical properties which have made asbestos so useful are:

* thermal stability and incombustibility
* thermal insulation (low thermal conductivity)
* electrical insulation
* tensile strength
* chemical durability and acid resistance.

It is variously estimated that around 3,000 products utilising asbestos have been produced, but little evidence is put forward to justify the claim. Nevertheless, it illustrates the versatility of asbestos, its great utility to humankind and its ability to be incorporated into a variety of matrices. The task of finding non-asbestos materials which can replace all the applications of asbestos has been extremely difficult. The alternatives are usually more expensive and often not as effective – and may still have hazards associated with their use.

Most of the asbestos applications used more than one of the properties, of course. For example, chrysotile fire blankets used the mechanical strength to allow it to be spun and woven into a textile with the thermal stability and insulation properties to resist the fire. In floor tiles, however, the sole purpose of the asbestos is to provide reinforcement of the tile.

The thermal properties have given asbestos its name, originally from a Greek word meaning "inextinguishable" – referring to the use of chrysotile for wicks for oil lamps, so that provided there was sufficient oil the wick would not burn down and the lamp was kept alight. In some European countries, however, asbestos is also referred to by words derived from the Greek "amiantos" – meaning "incorruptible" or "undefiled".

The thermal stability of asbestos extends up to about 600°C, although the various minerals show different responses and rates of degradation. Beyond these temperatures, asbestos starts to break down and lose its characteristic properties. Curiously, some of the replacement materials, particularly refractory ceramic fibres, have even better properties than asbestos.

The tensile strength of the three major asbestos types is about equivalent to that of stainless steel. It was used to give excellent reinforcement to a variety of matrices, such as cement sheet or pipes, thermoplastic floor tiles, insulating board, rubbers and plastics such as "Bakelite", as well as textiles and ropes where it could also have been blended with other natural or synthetic fibres. For the minor or rare types (anthophyllite, tremolite and actinolite) the tensile strength is very much lower and partly for this reason, these types have found less commercial use.

The acid resistance is quite distinct between the serpentine and amphibole asbestos minerals. In general, the amphiboles are far superior. If acid resistance were a critical property in an asbestos application, chrysotile would not have been used. Either amosite or crocidolite, or even tremolite, would have been preferred. Chrysotile is effectively destroyed by boiling in 50% hydrochloric acid for five to 10 minutes, since the external brucite (magnesium hydroxide) layer is very vulnerable.

For laboratory filtration purposes, older analytical chemists will remember "Gooch asbestos", which may have been a mixture of tremolite and anthophyllite. The Gooch crucibles had a perforated base, which was covered with a slurry of asbestos and then heated in a furnace at about 500°–600°C to produce the filter pad for a gravimetric analysis.

(Incidentally, and not related, home-made wine makers of the 1970s may remember that their kits were supplied with some chrysotile to filter the wine after fermentation!)

# Health effects and current trends

The distressing fact about asbestos is the range of fatal conditions that can be caused by exposure to airborne fibres. At least three major fatal diseases are recognised (asbestosis, lung cancer and mesothelioma) and several other conditions which are recognised but which are not so prevalent (or necessarily fatal), such as pleural plaques, cancer of the larynx, asbestos warts or corns. The three major fatal conditions are all notifiable diseases under RIDDOR. All of them have a long induction period – possibly up to several decades.

## *Asbestosis*

The adverse health effects of exposure to airborne asbestos fibres have been evident in the industrial age since the end of the 19th century, when there were reports by a lady inspector visiting an asbestos factory who found evidence of ill health and respiratory problems among the work force. She clearly made the link with the exposure to airborne asbestos fibres and the evidence of disease.

In the East End of London, in the early 1900s, Dr Montague Murray reported the death of a 33-year old man who had worked in an asbestos factory for 14 years. The post-mortem revealed the man's lungs to be hard and black and Montague Murray attributed his death to the man's occupational activity. The term "asbestosis" was first used in 1924, by which time the identity of the disease, its symptoms, causes and pathology had been clearly established. The term "asbestosis" was used to make the link with pneumoconiosis or silicosis in coal-miners, which had been established earlier in the late 19th century. The symptoms and pathology of the two diseases are very similar – crystalline quartz or silica in the coal dust, which contains about 5% silica, causes "miners' lung".

Parliament produced the first regulations in 1931 – the Asbestos Industries Regulations 1931 – but these were not well enforced and, indeed, were only aimed at the manufacturing premises, not at the end-user activities.

The disease is referred to as a fibrosis, in which the fibres produce a scarring of the lung tissue due to continual abrasion by the fibres as the lungs contract and expand. The scar tissue results in a loss of elasticity of the lungs and hence to loss of lung function. The characteristic picture is well known: a sufferer who can only exist with the permanent aid of an oxygen cylinder at their side. The disease progresses slowly in the early stages but may accelerate later. Its progress, however, will be inevitable. The first appearance of the disease may be within a matter of a few years in the case of very high exposures over an extended period, but may – perhaps more typically, now – appear not until 20 or many more years later if the exposure has been lower. In all cases the outcome is inevitably fatal. The ultimate cause of death may be due to pneumonia or heart disease, because the loss of lung function places extra strain on the cardiovascular system. In other cases, asbestosis may appear in conjunction with lung cancer or mesothelioma.

The HSE have recorded instances of the disease since the early 1970s and the picture of increasing incidence over the next two decades has been quite clear. The increase was clearly due to the large use of asbestos in the 1950s and 1960s. Because the usage declined in the 1970s, it might have been expected to result in a decrease in asbestosis deaths from the 1990s onwards, but the statistics show little sign yet of abating. Most of these deaths would have been among asbestos workers in factories, insulation workers in power stations and other industrial situations.

It is possible, however, that there are a number of deaths now occurring among the asbestos removal workers, some of whom may have installed the insulation in the first place. On the other hand, it is very unlikely that new exposures now occurring will lead to asbestosis in the future.

Asbestosis is normally regarded as an occupational disease for which industrial compensation is payable if there is a clear occupational exposure history. There are, however, many recorded cases where people have contracted the disease from a family member's contaminated clothing, ie outside the workplace. In other cases, it has been recognised that asbestosis can be caused among people living in moderately close proximity to an asbestos factory. (The same pattern is also seen in cases of mesothelioma.)

**Fig 4.4** UK Asbestosis deaths 1970–2000

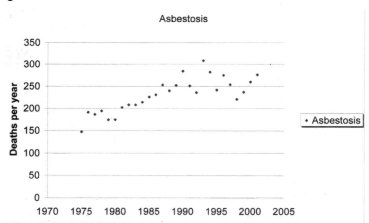

HSE statistics from www.hse.gov.uk/asbestos

## Lung cancer

The association of asbestos exposure with lung cancer was first established in about 1947 by the Annual Report of the Factory Inspector, highlighting the incidence of lung cancer among asbestos workers. It was later confirmed in a paper by Richard Doll in 1955 (Doll R "Mortality from lung cancer in asbestos workers" *British Journal of Industrial Medicine*, **12**, pp. 81–86). This should have come as no surprise because there is documentary evidence that the asbestos industry was already aware of the risk from their own personnel records in the 1920s and 1930s, and were doing as much as they could to keep the information from damaging their products (Tweedale G, *Magic Mineral to Killer Dust: Turner & Newall and the Asbestos Hazard* Oxford University Press, 2000). Part of the reason the link was so long in being established was, first, the confounding effect of smoking and, second, the relatively long induction or latency period which is usually at least 15 years but may be as long as 30 years or more.

The cancer is identical in many respects to the cancer caused by smoking tobacco products. It appears in the upper ciliated airways (as opposed to the alveoli mostly affected in asbestosis). The prognosis is never very good. If the tumour can be detected early it may removed surgically, but clearly it will mean the loss of a large section of the lung if not the whole lung. If the tumour has spread to both lungs, there is evidently a very serious outlook. Unfortunately, the tumour does not seem to respond well either to chemotherapy or to treatment with X-rays.

There is a clear and pronounced synergistic link with smoking. A smoker has a quantifiable risk of lung cancer and an asbestos worker also has a risk of lung cancer. If, however, the asbestos worker also smokes the risk of lung cancer is not just additive, it is greatly enhanced, by a factor of up to 50 times greater than a non-smoking non-asbestos worker. The effect is so great that an asbestos worker who smokes may have a 50% chance of contracting lung cancer.

The precise incidence of lung cancer from asbestos exposure in the UK is not easy to establish. Cases notified under RIDDOR depend on the medical practitioner or pathologist recognising the potential for asbestos-related lung cancer. It is not easy to diagnose pre-mortem, although sometimes sputum samples may show the characteristic marrowbone shaped bodies of asbestos fibres where the macrophages have unsuccessfully tried to engulf and eliminate the foreign bodies.

The HSE statistics show only about 400–500 cases per year, and for this reason, the HSE feel that lung cancer from asbestos only appears where there is sufficient exposure to cause asbestosis. However, they do recognise that probably many asbestos-related lung cancers go unrecognised and that there are probably between one and two excess lung cancer deaths per case of mesothelioma. This means we should be estimating about 2,000–3,000 lung cancers per year related to asbestos. The total number of deaths due to lung cancer in the UK is about 35,000 per year, the vast majority of which would be related to smoking, so about one in 12 to 15 lung cancer cases are asbestos-related.

The recent studies by Darnton and Hodgson and by Berman and Crump (for the US Environmental Protection Agency) indicate that the amphiboles are more significant for lung cancer than chrysotile by a factor of about 10–50 times. This is much less than the corresponding ratios for mesothelioma (see below).

## Mesothelioma

The third of these diseases is very specific to asbestos. It is a normally rare tumour of the pleural membrane surrounding the lungs or of the peritoneal cavity. The link with asbestos exposure was first established by Chris Wagner in South Africa (JC Wagner *et al.* (1960) "Diffuse pleural mesothelioma and asbestos exposure in North Western Cape Province" *British Journal of Industrial Medicine* **17** pp 260–271). He was looking at cases (thought initially to be tuberculosis) among the local population around the crocidolite mines. He was able to establish that this was actually mesothelioma, which until then was a relatively unknown disease.

The tumour produces a thick growth around the lungs, which can extend throughout the chest cavity and even penetrate the rib cage if drainage points have been put in to remove excess fluid. By the time the diagnosis is made, it is, sadly, too late. As for all the other asbestos diseases, the latency or induction period is very long, probably at least 15 years and more probably 20–40 years, or even longer. Mesothelioma rarely appears before the age of 40 and is much more likely to appear in the 60s and 70s. Cases appearing before the age of about 40 may well be due to childhood exposure – from a father's dirty work overalls or from living near an asbestos factory, for example.

Because of the nature of the tumour, surgery is not usually an option, but there have been at least a couple of cases where surgery has been tried, but the outcome is not recorded. It is a very painful death and a thoroughly unpleasant disease for all concerned. The life expectancy after diagnosis is probably no more than nine to 18 months at most. There is very little effective treatment available. There has been some recent work on anti-cancer drugs, using the same type of drugs or cocktail of drugs as used for treating breast cancer. The higher profile of mesothelioma may stimulate development of more effective therapies.

The principal causative agents have been shown to be the amphiboles. The risk factors have been assessed as 500:100:1 for crocidolite:amosite:chrysotile. In other words, chrysotile is 500 times less dangerous than crocidolite. Indeed, some sources (particularly those in the chrysotile production areas) suggest that chrysotile does not cause mesothelioma at all. They suggest that a well-known and much quoted study at a North Carolina mill showing case(s) of mesothelioma in a chrysotile weaving factory were largely (if not solely) because the factory had used crocidolite for a brief period. However, a further factor to consider is that chrysotile sometimes contains traces of tremolite, one of the rarer amphibole asbestos minerals, and it may be that the causative agent is the tremolite and not the chrysotile. The presence of tremolite may well be very significant and some of the current thinking is that tremolite is an even more potent agent for mesothelioma than crocidolite.

There have been two other (possible) causes of mesothelioma identified, a SV40 virus and erionite, a mineral in the Anatolia region of Turkey. The SV40 virus (a simian immuno-virus) was first identified in mesothelioma tissue in about 2000 (Rizzo, Carbone, Fisher, *et al. Chest* 1999 **116** pp 470S–473S), and it is thought to have originated from contamination in the first human (injectable) polio vaccines in the 1950s or 1960s – but not the later oral vaccines. If that is the case, then might we expect to see a major incidence of mesothelioma in the UK from about 2000–2020?

The erionite in Turkey is a natural zeolite mineral, a moderately soft rock, which also produces respirable fibres. In this region, the local inhabitants have burrowed into a cliff face to create workshops and storage facilities, and if they want to expand, they simply burrow a bit deeper. Because of erosion of the soft erionite, there is a natural local incidence of mesothelioma in the population.

With both the cancers, we might expect to see some genetic link, as we already see in some other cancers such as breast cancer. Two studies are of particular interest. First, a recent study (Roushdy-Hammady *et al. Lancet* 2002 **357** pp 444–445) has indeed identified genetic links to the susceptibility to mesothelioma amongst the local inhabitants in Anatolia. Second, a recent study has shown that lung cancer among smokers also has a genetic link and it would not take a great leap to expect to find the same kind of link for asbestos workers and lung cancer. This might help to explain why some people have worked for significant periods with asbestos with little or no signs of ill effects, whereas others have contracted mesothelioma from a relatively small exposure. In many cases it is very difficult to see where the exposure has occurred in the first place.

The incidence of mesothelioma in the UK has been of great concern over the last decade. In 1986, the HSE fully expected mesothelioma to start to decline after about 1991 or so, because crocidolite was not used after 1969 when a trade ban was agreed in the UK. The HSE were duly horrified when Professor Julian Peto reviewed the mesothelioma rates in 1995 (Peto, Hodgson, Matthews, Jones, *Lancet* 1995 **345** pp 535–539) and they concluded that the situation required action to prevent further exposure of workers who may accidentally disturb asbestos in buildings. The current HSE view is that mesothelioma rates will not be expected to peak and then start to decline until somewhere between 2011 and 2015. By then, of course, up to 3,000–4,000 cases of mesothelioma per year may be expected, a truly horrendous prospect. HSE are officially expecting mesotheliomas to peak between 1,950 to 2,450 cases per year, but there is no expectation as to how fast the rates will decline once it has peaked.

The extent of the problem is clearly shown in Fig 4.5. In the mid 1980s, when the HSE expected mesotheliomas to peak in the early 1990s, the death rate was about 600 per year. By the time Professor Peto gave them the bad news in 1995, it had already climbed to 1,200 per year, and that figure had reached 1,848 per year by 2001. The true picture may be worse than shown here because it is possible that the mesothelioma rates in the early 1970s were understated. Some mesothelioma cases may not have been recognised and simply classified as lung cancer. Without doubt, however, the longer life expectancy for males, which has increased by 10 years over the last half century, has contributed to the ability of mesothelioma to develop late in life.

One of the problems is that a relatively smaller exposure may cause the disease and there is a suggestion that cumulative low-level exposures may be just as harmful as a briefer higher-level exposure. It is clear that it is mainly an occupational disease since the death rates are biased about 6:1 for male:female deaths. The exposure occurs normally in those trades traditionally occupied by male workers, although there was an interesting study of women producing gas masks in World War II (Acheson, Gardner, Pippard, Grime (1983) *British Journal of Industrial Medicine* **39** pp 344–348) where the filters were made of crocidolite. Mesothelioma (and other asbestos-related diseases) in women has also been frequently identified where wives have laundered their husbands' asbestos-contaminated overalls.

**Fig 4.5** Asbestos related deaths 1975–2001

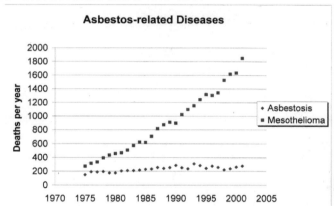

Data from HSE web site; http://www.hse.gov.uk/statistics/causdis/meso.htm

However, some light at the end of the tunnel was seen late in 2003. Two groups of researchers in Australia and USA (Robinson, Creaney, Lake, *et al Lancet* 2003 **362** pp 1612–1616) had been able to detect a soluble mesothelin-related protein (SMR) in blood samples, possibly indicative of the early onset of mesothelioma. The hope then would be that the tumour could be treated before diagnosis was made from the appearance of other symptoms. Treatment with chemotherapy or radiation therapy could possibly be more effective and give a better chance of successful treatment.

# Applications of Asbestos in Buildings

## Introduction

There are many materials where asbestos has been used in building products and in the built environment. A figure of 3,000 products with asbestos is often quoted, but it is difficult to find any supporting documentation for this claim.

Many of these materials are known by their trade names, but essentially the same material from different manufacturers may be given different names. There is a useful web site provided by the Asbestos Information Centre at www.aic.org.uk with a collection of some of the most well known materials, dates of manufacture, compositions and trade names.

Some materials are referred to below by their common names, but over time, and with the disappearance of the asbestos manufacturing industry, it is sometimes difficult to establish the correct name for a specific material.

The classification below is a series of typical products, but this should not be regarded as exclusive. Surveyors will often come across materials which do not appear to fit into any of these categories, and indeed do not appear to be a building material as such, simply just an application of asbestos. Surveyors should, of course, be including asbestos in fixtures and fittings (rope seals on ovens and furnaces, insulation panels in electrical heaters, flash guards in fuses, etc) in their survey report.

The composition and application of these materials is not unequivocal. In this part of the field, words like "never" and "always" should be avoided. Surveyors and analysts will often be able to find exceptions to practically every statement.

## Sprayed coatings

Sprayed coatings were used in the UK from the 1930s through to the mid-1970s. Much of these coatings have now been removed but there are still examples to be found in some older, less well-maintained buildings. Sprayed crocidolite was installed to about 1969 (when the industry ban on crocidolite came into place) and amosite and chrysotile were reported to have been used up to about 1974. However, it is suggested that in a very few cases, sprayed asbestos coatings may have been used as late as 1978 or 1979.

There were three main applications:

• Fire protection of structural steelwork
  The coating could be anything from about 50 mm to 150 mm thick, depending on the fire rating required.

• Anti-condensation coatings
  These coatings would be rather thinner, usually not more than about 25 mm thick, used for example in swimming pools and school kitchens. (In swimming pools, the sprayed coating served a dual purpose – anti-condensation and acoustic attenuation.) (Fig 5.1)

• Acoustic attenuation
  The asbestos is simply to provide an acoustic treatment, and so was used in areas such as cinemas and theatres, and was also found in some Magistrates' Courts.

As the name suggests, it was applied by spraying, although in some cases it was also trowelled on. The composition would usually have been from about 55%–85% w/w asbestos (mostly the higher levels) with a cement binder, sprayed on as a wet slurry. The original spraying process sometimes included a preliminary coating of an adhesive layer such as bitumen, which later makes it very difficult to

**Fig 5.1** Swimming pool ceiling with sprayed asbestos (amosite and chrysotile) underneath a corrugated asbestos cement roof. Although the coating is encapsulated, note the water damage at the left from rainwater penetration.

remove the asbestos completely. Naturally, the spraying was a very messy process and it is usual to find "overspray" onto adjacent surfaces, into crevices and behind shuttering. If the surveyor suspects a sprayed coating has been previously removed (and resprayed with a non-asbestos replacement material), he must be on the alert for these residues.

The compositions fall into four main types:

- crocidolite
- amosite
- mixed amosite and chrysotile
- chrysotile.

There is a reference in older publications to a crocidolite coating with an over-coating of chrysotile, but this must have been very rare and any examples would now be very unlikely to be found. Sprayed chrysotile on its own is relatively unusual in the UK and most of the crocidolite sprayed coatings have been removed over the last 15 years. The majority of the remaining coatings are therefore based on either amosite or mixed amosite and chrysotile.

This material is often generically referred to as "Limpet" but strictly this refers to a Turner & Newall product, which apparently was never based on crocidolite.

Unsealed sprayed coatings are low density, very soft and friable, easily damaged by abrasion, by birds (to take as a nesting material) and vermin, or by water from a leaking roof, for example. They will often be found with a paint seal or encapsulated with a cloth which has been soaked in a proprietary sealant and wrapped around the coated beam. The cloth coating is suitable for areas that are likely to be occupied. Any accidental abrasion (provided it is not excessive) should not cause any significant fibre release.

Non-asbestos coatings are also found, based on materials such as fibreglass or vermiculite ("Mandoval" or "Mandolite"). These are also soft, but more modern materials are based on pulverised fuel ash (PFA) with cement and make a very hard coating which looks like "breeze block" – essentially the same composition. The soft coatings based on fibre glass or vermiculite appear very similar to the amosite or chrysotile sprayed coatings and the surveyor is unlikely to be able to distinguish them reliably without analysis.

# Thermal insulation to pipe-work and vessels

Of all the asbestos materials seen, this class presents the greatest variation of types and compositions. Pipe insulation must be treated with caution and should be inspected carefully along its length. Depending on its age, there may be many different types of materials even within a single plant room because of repairs or extensions to the pipework over its lifetime. It would be common to find mixtures of insulation materials on the same pipe run, and surveyors need to check the whole length of the pipe insulation, particularly elbows and any repairs.

The terms lagging and insulation are used here interchangeably. The term "lagging" refers to the material itself as well as to the process of applying the material to the pipe or vessel.

**Fig 5.2** Pipe to be stripped. This pipe is about to be stripped when the boiler is replaced in the next month. It could have been repaired and encapsulated if necessary, however.

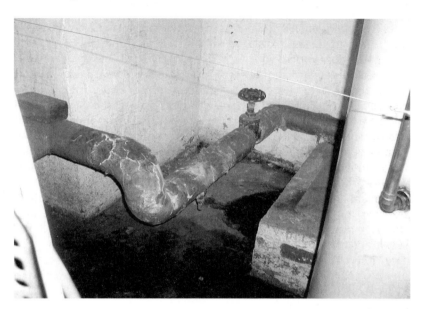

Asbestos composition insulation was probably not used after about 1974, although the chrysotile paper based products (see p 59) may have been used later.

The main types of insulation materials can be classified as follows.

## Composition

This would have been made up on site from a dry material, mixed with water in a large tub or bath to a workable consistency, then applied wet to the pipework by hand. There may be more than one layer, perhaps separated by a layer of chicken-wire. The layers of the insulation may well be very different and it is not unusual to find non-asbestos and asbestos materials together. Repairs to the insulation would be made with whatever was available to the lagger, including the recycling of old insulation.

The external surface may be a hard-set plaster or cement, painted cloth or, if it is external, a layer of roofing felt as a waterproof covering, held in place with metal straps or chicken-wire.

The asbestos content of these materials is highly variable and unpredictable, and the total content could be up to about 60–70%, based on any combination of all the asbestos minerals, with the exception of actinolite. It would be very unusual, however, to find more than three asbestos types together. On the other hand, very old pipe insulation can be seen with just a trace amount of asbestos, including traces of the rarer types (anthophyllite or tremolite) perhaps mixed with other fibres, such as wood fibre, cellulose and animal hair.

It is reported that the laggers used to incorporate a small amount of crocidolite in the outer layer to help the water to drain off because of the hydrophobic properties of the amphibole asbestos minerals.

The application of these materials was a quite a skill and in the power stations was an apprenticed trade. Later, many of these men would be involved with the removal of the insulation they had installed in the first place.

## Pre-formed sectional insulation

The most common form is "Caposite", a material based on amosite, made by Cape Asbestos. This is formed in semi-circular sections, with an external cloth covering and held in place by metal straps. It had a very high asbestos content, invariably amosite, up to about 65%. Because it is pre-formed, it is obviously suitable only for the pipe diameter for which it is made.

The elbows of the pipework may be left bare, or alternatively, insulated with either chrysotile rope or composition material. This is particularly the case where the sectional material is based on man-made fibre (fibreglass, rockwood, slagwool, refractory ceramic fibre (RCF)). They are also known as MMVF or man-made vitreous fibres. These are quite distinct from asbestos since they are not crystalline materials and do not have the same hazardous properties. However, they should be regarded with caution.

## Glass-fibre insulation lined with chrysotile paper

A common product applied to steam mains pipes is glass fibre (with a roofing felt and chicken wire outer layer) but the lowest layer is chrysotile paper as an anti-corrosion protection for the steel pipe. It is not clear whether the chrysotile paper was incorporated into the pre-formed insulation or applied separately as an under-layer.

## Chrysotile paper

This material looks rather similar to corrugated cardboard, but made entirely of chrysotile and usually with an aluminium foil backing. It was used mainly in applications such as a lining to boiler casing or in heater cupboards, but it can also be found used as pipe insulation, wrapped around the pipe.

## Sectional felt insulation lined with chrysotile paper

This insulation was used on low-pressure steam lines, heating or hot water pipes. It consists of layered grey or brown felt – mixed vegetable fibre and animal hair fibres – with an inner layer (1–2 mm) of chrysotile paper. The whole material is covered with a cloth layer and the semi-circular sections held together with metal straps. It appears both with and without the paper liner; the chrysotile paper lined type would be for the "steam" or hot side and the unlined type would be for the "condensate" or return pipes. However, the laggers (or repairers) would have used whatever was available, so it is quite possible to find lined and unlined sections on the same pipe run.

## "Cork and Keenes"

Keenes cement was a white hard-set finish used to seal pipe insulation, applied as a layer of about 2–6 mm thickness. It was also used on sectional cork insulation for cold water pipes and on slabs of cork insulation on cold-water storage tanks. It was nominally based on gypsum (calcium sulphate or plaster) but it has been found to contain amosite and chrysotile. It has also been seen as an external coating on sectional mineral wool insulation.

Later non-asbestos insulation materials were based on cellulose/ vegetable fibre and/or glass fibre, either as pre-formed sectional materials or wet-mix materials. Even where these materials are intended to be non-asbestos, they may have been applied after a poor quality strip of the original asbestos and may therefore conceal debris, or they may have been mixed with asbestos residues in the initial application.

**Fig 5.3** Part of an old boiler house (now demolished) which illustrates the typical range of insulation materials to be found in such locations

# Mill-boards

Mill-boards are very soft, low-density boards (probably less than 500 kg/m³) with a high asbestos content, often used in electrical equipment to provide thermal insulation or fire protection. They were based on any of the three major types of asbestos, with starch or clay as the binder.

**Fig 5.4** Wood acoustic enclosure, lined with millboard, around motor and fan for a church organ. (Note the flexible collar around the fan exhaust which also contains asbestos.)

# Asbestos insulating board (AIB)

This very common product was marketed under a range of trade names, the most well-known of which is "Asbestolux". Indeed, that trade name is a now used as a generic name for this type of material. AIB was used in a variety of applications where thermal insulation or fire protection was required within a building, but also where someone needed a simple piece of sheet material for packing or shuttering.

The purpose of the asbestos is to provide both thermal insulation and mechanical reinforcement. AIB is referred to as a semi-compressed board, based on a Portland cement matrix, in several distinct asbestos compositions (in order of frequency of occurrence):

- amosite
- amosite with a small proportion of chrysotile
- crocidolite and chrysotile.

The total amount of asbestos would be in the range 15%–30% but some of the earlier boards, (when asbestos was cheaper) could have been up to 40%. The density of these boards would normally have been about 700 kg/m³, but some other boards could have a density of up to 1,400 kg/m³. Where the board density is greater than 1,000 kg/m³, under the Asbestos (Licensing) Regulations 1983 it should be classified as asbestos cement and not therefore subject to the requirements of these regulations. The guidance (in HSE's L11 – A guide to the Asbestos (Licensing) Regulations 1983) suggests that where there is doubt about its classification a density measurement should be made, but it is widely recognised that this measurement is not easy to do with any accuracy and the definition is clearly open to abuse by unscrupulous unlicensed contractors. It is very probable that when the Asbestos (Licensing) Regulations are revised, the density definition will disappear and be replaced by a measurement based on water absorption.

These boards were being made in the UK up to about 1980 although the finished products were still being imported up to 1985 when the amosite and crocidolite were finally prohibited. AIB was certainly being installed in new buildings up to this date. Old stock, recycled or salvage AIB materials may occasionally be found being used even later.

Because the panels are relatively much softer than asbestos cement, it is possible to nail sheets to battens, but more frequently these panels would be drilled and screwed to the supporting frame.

The principal applications were:

- ceiling tiles and skylight upstands
- wall panels, possibly as a sandwich construction
- fire breaks above suspended ceilings
- ventilation ducting – both extract and supply ducts – including warm air ducted central heating systems
- riser panels and boxing around services
- soffits for eaves, porches and walkways
- uprating of protection on fire doors
- fire protection for plant room ceilings.

**Fig 5.5** Asbestos insulating board as fire stop within a riser in a 1960s office block.

Other applications include glazing strips to partitions and fire door vision panels. As sheet material, it is also seen laminated with formica sheet as a riser panel in toilets, for example.

The majority of the AIB applications were internal since its weather resistance is limited. The only external applications would be as soffits, ie downward facing surfaces, under eaves, porches and walkways, where it would be protected from the elements.

# Asbestos cement products

Asbestos cement (AC) products manufactured in the early 1980s accounted for more than one third of imported chrysotile. AC is a dense, hard material with good weather and water resistance. It is perhaps the most commonly found of asbestos applications, mostly because of the durability of the product. AC sheets will usually have a service life of more than 30 years – and, in favourable conditions, probably a good deal longer. In the UK, AC sheet products (including corrugated sheet) were being manufactured and installed right up to 1999 when virtually all the remaining chrysotile products were finally prohibited.

Most sheet and profiled material was based on chrysotile and contains about 12%–15% by weight. It is fully compressed and usually has a density of about 1,600–1,900 kg/m$^3$. Some products contain small amounts of crocidolite (~1%) as well as the usual chrysotile. Amosite or crocidolite was added for technical reasons in moulded products such as tanks and hoppers. The hydrophobic amphibole helped the water to drain off more rapidly and thus speeded up the production of these products. Crocidolite is found added more often than amosite but occasionally it is possible to find all three major types together. Some examples of water supply pressure pipes contain large amounts of crocidolite, with the fibres appearing unusually coarse. There are also rare examples of sheet AC material based on amosite rather than chrysotile.

One interesting example (unusual but not rare) is cement slates or tiles with chrysotile and significant amounts of tremolite. Normally, these slates or tiles would have been based on chrysotile alone.

The main products to be seen are:

- profiled and flat sheets
- moulded ridge tiles, barge boards
- cement slates or cladding tiles
- promenade or decking tiles
- rainwater goods:
  - gutters
  - down-pipes
  - hoppers
- water supply pressure pipes
- cold water storage tanks.

Cold water storage tanks were extensively used in housing after World War II, possibly into the 1970s, in private housing as well as local authority housing estates. It was used as a replacement for galvanised steel, which was in short supply after the war.

There were also some decorative panel materials, including notably a dark grey or black product known as "Massal" from Eternit, used as window boards and also a white version for external window sills. The black window boards are commonly found in schools, in offices and in domestic premises. It is found as two forms, either textured to look like slate, or as a shiny, polished surface, and in each case the board is about 15mm thick. It was probably used until the late 1970s or early 1980s.

The infill panels found beneath windows were also a cement material and one trade name used for this was "Glasal".

# Textiles, ropes and paper

Spun and woven materials were some of the earliest asbestos applications, because chrysotile was the first asbestos type to be imported and because of the suitability of chrysotile for this application. Initially, chrysotile was spun with a cellulose fibre to aid the spinning and examples are seen where chrysotile is blended with other synthetic organic fibres, but other materials are based on chrysotile alone.

The spun materials were produced in a range of thickness, from a string up to heavy gauge ropes about 15 mm diameter. It was also produced as a graphitised material for caulking.

Because chrysotile is a serpentine mineral, its flexibility is quite distinct from that of the amphiboles. Although spun and woven crocidolite materials are seen (used particularly for jackets on steam locomotive boilers, or boiler rope seals, for example), they are much less common and the equivalent amosite products are very rarely seen.

Ropes would have been used as seals where heat insulation and fire protection is required, around flues or pipes where they pass through a wall or partition, around a window frame as a fire stop, or around an oven or furnace door.

Asbestos paper is almost solely based on pure chrysotile without any other non-asbestos materials added. The corrugated paper referred to above was used in heater cupboards and particularly as a lining to the casing of large domestic boilers.

Chrysotile flash guards for re-wirable electrical fuses were widely used and are still seen in use in many instances.

Fire blankets and asbestos gloves were mostly removed from use and replaced with non-asbestos equivalents in the 1980s and 1990s. It is surprising therefore to see so many still in place.

Chrysotile paper was also used as a facing to other non-asbestos boards. There is a board referred to as "flame retardant insulating board" (FRIB) which was used as ceiling and wall panels (and even as pin-boards in schools). It was a lightweight cellulose board with a thin chrysotile paper coating. Another type of board (with a trade name of "Strammit") was essentially a strawboard for ceiling panels, but sometimes found with a chrysotile paper coating.

# Floor tiles and coverings

## Thermoplastic tiles

Thermoplastic tiles were widely produced with asbestos (chrysotile) added as reinforcement. These were manufactured and installed until the 1970s, and contain only chrysotile, but very rarely also seen with anthophyllite. The adhesive could also contain asbestos (see later) but in some cases, it has been suggested that in the production process, the tiles were dusted with chrysotile before being stacked to prevent them sticking to each other and hence the presence of the asbestos in the adhesive.

## Vinyl floor coverings (eg Novilon)

Some vinyl floor coverings have a chrysotile paper backing which acts as a cushion. It was commonly used in domestic premises, in kitchens and lobbies, usually on a solid concrete floor and may (or may not) have been laid with an adhesive. In this case, when the flooring was removed, the asbestos layer would remain on the floor and prove very difficult to remove.

# Gaskets, joints and packing

CAF (Compressed asbestos fibre) gaskets were produced late into the 1990s. They are comprised almost exclusively of chrysotile, with a small amount of binder.

Gland packing for valve stems was based on chrysotile. Two forms of "Indurated asbestos" were produced; blue and red, both dyed chrysotile, with a binder added to make a firm seal. (It is natural to think that blue "indurated asbestos" was crocidolite but it was actually dyed chrysotile and the end product looked nothing like raw crocidolite!)

# Putties, mastics and adhesives

These materials are not frequently seen with asbestos, but chrysotile was sometimes added to these materials. It is reportedly also found in putties used for steel framed windows. Some floor tile adhesives are found with chrysotile, even where the floor tile itself appears to be non-asbestos.

# Composite bonded materials

There are a number of products where asbestos was used in a variety of products.

## *Wallboard D, Partition board*

This is a cement-based board, with high content of cellulose (wood) fibre but also with about 5% asbestos added. There are two main versions, with either chrysotile or a mixture of chrysotile and crocidolite. It is a very hard, dense, rigid material, yellowish or brown in colour, about 3 mm thick, produced in sheets. It was used for walls and partitions in temporary buildings and caravans, but also in fume-cupboards and infill panels behind gas fires. It has also been used for partitions in low-cost housing in tower blocks.

## *Durasteel*

A sandwich material with amosite board between two sheets of perforated steel, used as a fire door, fireproof partitions or infill panels above doors. The overall thickness would be about 15–30 mm.

## *"Belgium board"*

(There is some uncertainty about this trade name.)

A dense chipboard or blockboard faced on both sides with a thin (2 or 3 mm) layer of conventional asbestos cement sheet. The overall thickness of the panel is about 30–40 mm. This material was produced in large sheets about 2.5m × 1.5 m, and used as partitions in office buildings.

## *Slates or tiles*

Asbestos was used in two main ways. It was found as straightforward asbestos cement tiles (referred to above), used as either roof tiles or cladding, and these were being used as early as the 1930s. Another form, however, was reconstituted slate, where slate dust was compressed with chrysotile fibre. They can be recognised by straight, sharp, clean edges, compared with real slate. These slates were much cheaper than the genuine article but not so durable and the replacement non-asbestos slates were even less durable.

# Friction products, brakes and clutches

Not normally regarded as a building product, but found in lift motor rooms as brake shoes. These would not normally be sampled, but there may be stocks of replacement shoes stored ready for use. They would have been based on a phenolic resin and would only have contained chrysotile (30%–70%).

# Plastics
## *Toilet cisterns*

The most common type was the "Shires Lynx" range. They were made of black Bakelite reinforced with (usually) amosite, but also found with chrysotile and/or crocidolite. These are very durable and there are still many examples of these to be found in use today. Presumably, the corresponding toilet seats would also have been made of the same material, but these would have been replaced much more frequently.

## *Electrical fittings*

There are examples of junction boxes made of Bakelite reinforced with asbestos.

# Textured or decorative coatings
## *"Artex" and other trade names*

Decorative coatings were very popular in the 1960s right through to the 1980s and later. They were initially based on small amounts of chrysotile to provide some bulk and reinforcement. The amount of asbestos ranged from about 0.5% w/w to 3% w/w but sometimes with very short, fine fibres, which makes the chrysotile difficult to detect in the sample.

No other types of asbestos are believed to have been used, although if the coating has been applied to a ceiling of AIB, for example, it is very possible that the sampling will pick up amosite fibres from the substrate. (The AIB would need to have been sealed before the textured coating was applied, as it would have been too absorbent.)

**Fig 5.6** Textured coating of unknown age – non-asbestos

The surveyor will not be able to recognise on site whether the coating contains asbestos or not. This will have to be confirmed by sampling and analysis.

Textured coating materials were supplied as a powder and mixed up with water on site. The non-asbestos equivalents were based usually on mica-type minerals and were available from the early 1980s, so there was an overlap period of several years where both asbestos and non-asbestos versions were available on the market. Those who applied these materials, however, preferred the asbestos type and it would be very common to find mixed materials on site.

These materials were finally prohibited in 1988, but stocks were in the supply chain in the early 1990s and some was found in a DIY depot stock room as late as 1999.

# Acoustic attenuation
## *"Paxfelt"*

Acoustic attenuator panels were made with loose asbestos (almost 100% mixed amosite and chrysotile) as a sandwich between wire mesh panels. The whole attenuator would be about 25 mm thick and placed within a ventilation duct. On the bends it may be possible to see where the air currents have scoured out the surface of the asbestos.

Asbestos was also used a loose fill in floor cavities for sound attenuation between flats, for example.

# Bituminous products (roofing felt, DPC, etc)
## *"Galbestos"*

Corrugated iron sheets with a chrysotile paper coating impregnated with bitumen. This was sometimes also known as RPM – Robinson's Profiled Metal. It was used mostly for industrial buildings and the purpose of the bitumen/chrysotile paper was simply as an anti-corrosion protection, replacing the zinc galvanising process.

## Damp Proof Course (DPC) ("Astos")

A 2 mm thick bitumen based material reinforced with vegetable and chrysotile fibre.

## Roofing felt

This was a similar product to the DPC and used for flat roofs. It should be distinguished from the sarking felt used on a pitched roof. The material was banned from January 1993 in the Asbestos (Prohibitions) Regulations 1992.

## Acoustic sink pads

Stainless steel sinks often have a bituminous pad under either the bowl or drainer (or both) as acoustic treatment. Naturally, there are non-asbestos versions found.

# Age of the building

This chapter has indicated how products have been introduced and phased out over many decades. The age of the building being surveyed is a crucial piece of information and may indeed indicate that it really does not need to be surveyed if it is later than about 1993. It may contain some asbestos cement or possibly some asbestos gaskets or roofing felt but these are all low risk materials.

The information above has tried to include dates when these materials would have been phased out. For example, it would be possible to indicate what materials would be likely to be found in a building of a known age, for example:

| Date built | Materials possibly present |
|---|---|
| 2003 | (none?) |
| 1993 | Asbestos cement products, roofing felt, gaskets |
| 1983 | Asbestos insulating board, textured coatings – plus the above |
| 1973 | Asbestos insulation, sprayed asbestos coatings, floor tiles – plus all of the above |

These dates can only be indications because there was often an overlap of several years between the introduction of new non-asbestos alternative products and the disappearance of the equivalent asbestos material. It is certain that old stocks of some materials were used beyond the dates they should have been withdrawn, either from material in stock or in the supply chain, or as salvage materials being recycled. These dates, therefore, need to be treated with caution.

# Survey Types and Purposes

## CAWR 2002

### Regulation 4 – Duty to manage

The principal objective of the new regulations in 2002 was to introduce the new "duty to manage" asbestos in non-domestic premises. Although this was the first time this duty had appeared in the regulations, it had already been implicit under the HSWA 1974 and even more specifically under the Management of Health and Safety at Work Regulations 1992 (later amended and reissued in 1999).

## HSWA 1974

The provisions that are relevant include:

> sections 2 and 3 – duty of an employer to protect the health and safety of employees and others who visit or occupy their premises for whatever reason

In other words, to ensure that asbestos materials are kept in a safe condition and occupants and others are prevented from damaging it, exposing themselves and others to asbestos.

> section 4 – duty of an employer or owner of the premises to keep it in a safe condition

This is the duty to maintain premises, access and exits in a safe condition.

The main activities likely to release airborne asbestos fibres in buildings are:

- Accidental disturbance of asbestos containing materials (ACMs) during normal occupation activities by abrasion, impact, water damage, etc.
- Low frequency vibration from machinery on the softer boards or on insulation materials.
- Minor maintenance work on the building fabric and services.
- Major refurbishment or demolition where the structure and fabric is to be substantially disturbed.

In addition, some of the soft, friable materials have little mechanical strength and exposure to water or moisture will accelerate the natural deterioration: these materials will have a limited service life.

From the point of view of the surveyor, two of the essential components of regulation 4 are:

Para 4(b)

> ... the condition of any asbestos which is, or has been assumed to be, present in the premises shall be considered.

It is clearly not sufficient simply to locate the ACMs. Their condition needs to be assessed so that the dutyholder can arrange for any damage to be repaired or any debris to be cleaned up as soon as practicable – or access prevented. Alternatively, the ACM may need to be removed safely if it is beyond economic repair or liable to be damaged further.

This means that the surveyor will need to agree a condition assessment protocol with the client. In practice, this will probably· follow the materials risk assessment described in Methods for the Determination of Hazardous Substances (MDHS) 100 (para 61 and Table 2) and HSG 227 (Appendix 2): see also the discussion in chapter 7 below.

Para 5(b)

> ... an inspection is made of those parts of the premises which are reasonably accessible.

This level of access will need to be agreed with the dutyholder. "Reasonably accessible" will mean something different for the two levels of survey, Types 1 and 2 or Type 3. For a Type 3 survey, the level of access required is much higher and presumption of asbestos in a material will be much less acceptable in the final result.

## ACoP L127

Regulation 4 of CAWR 2002 is very comprehensive and detailed. L127 is therefore necessary to provide some guidance on what would be required to demonstrate compliance with the regulation.

L127 makes it clear both in the ACoP and in the accompanying guidance that the survey and assessment procedures in MDHS 100 are what is expected of the surveyor. However, this appears only in the ACoP – not the regulation – and is therefore not a statutory requirement. Although not yet interpreted by the courts, as with any prosecution under Health and Safety Regulations, it would be open to a defendant to show that he had used an equivalent or better set of procedures to comply with the regulations. For all practical purposes, however, there is no other guidance in the public domain which has undergone the appropriate level of scrutiny and validation, so MDHS 100 is recognised as the standard to be followed.

## MDHS 100 – Guidance for surveyors

MDHS 100 is the HSE's principal guidance for surveyors for asbestos materials in buildings. It is also guidance for clients or anyone who commissions a surveyor to inspect a building for asbestos materials. It was developed by the HSE committee Working Group 2 (WG2), itself a sub-committee of HSE's Committee on Fibre Measurement (CFM). The driving force for its production was largely a response to the poor quality of surveys, reports and registers seen by HSE inspectors out on site. MDHS 100 brought together some of the best of practices by the established consultancies to try and raise the quality level of asbestos surveys.

It is a very useful document, and not simply for the plentiful illustrations of a range of asbestos materials, both the conventional and some rather more unusual ACMs. For the first time, it defined the three types of surveys in terms that are now common parlance.

These definitions should be clearly understood, together with the limitations of each. The distinction is critical for clients, so that they fully understand the application of each type and commission the surveyor accordingly.

## Survey types (Type 1, 2 and 3) defined in MDHS 100

### Access (Type 1 and 2)

The building structure must be thoroughly examined and potential ACMs noted. It is required to gain access to all cavities and voids so far as is reasonably practicable, including ceiling voids, loft spaces, risers and floor ducts. Where it is agreed that it is not reasonably practicable to access and inspect any area, this must be unambiguously indicated in the survey report. Examples of lack of access could include:

(i) Situations where excessive damage to the fabric and decorations might be caused:
  • suspended ceiling tiles nailed on timber battens (screwed tiles may possibly be removed without excessive damage)
  • timber cladding to an internal partition which cannot be easily removed
  • no key available for a locked door, hatch or duct cover
  • external cladding tiles over a suspected ACM
  • decorative coating in domestic premises.

(ii) Situations where safety considerations prevent access at the time of the survey, due to:
  • working at height
  • confined spaces – and no safe procedures for access are in place
  • other chemical or physical hazards.

(iii) Situations where the client requires no access by the surveyor:
  • high security areas
  • operational or technical reasons.

In all these situations, it must be clearly indicated that no access was gained and asbestos must be presumed to be present in these areas. The client must be advised to not undertake any work here unless these have been investigated thoroughly.

## Type 1 – Location and assessment (presumption of asbestos)

A Type 1 survey is a non-sampling presumptive survey. Obviously, because no samples are taken for confirmation, the surveyor must presume that materials which cannot clearly be identified as non-asbestos (for example, brick, wood or metal) will have to be presumed to contain asbestos, unless there is a strongly reasoned argument to the contrary. Even here, surveyors need to be very cautious about materials concealed behind anything that appears to be non-asbestos. In any case, composites of rubbers or plastics may be manufactured with asbestos reinforcing (eg bakelite toilet cisterns). MDHS 100 emphasizes that a surveyor must have strong evidence for a reasoned argument for presuming that a material does not contain asbestos.

A material that cannot be recognised as non-asbestos is either "presumed" or "strongly presumed":

Presumed:

> the material is not necessarily recognised and cannot be categorically classified as non-asbestos so must be presumed by default to contain asbestos.

Strongly presumed:

> asbestiform fibres can be seen at a broken edge of the material or in the material itself, or
> the material is recognised as a known or typical ACM, or
> other very similar materials in this site have been analysed and found to contain asbestos.

Supporting evidence could be taken from other characteristics such as surface texture, warmth to the touch, sound when knocked and surface hardness when carefully tested with some kind of hand tool (bradawl, screwdriver or knife).

It is clear that the presumption or strong presumption of asbestos has to err on the side of caution and that presumption may well prove to be wrong. The client should understand that a Type 1 survey, which may be quicker and cheaper initially, may in the longer term prove to be a more expensive option. Almost certainly, if work is to be done later on "presumed" materials, sampling and analysis will be required. Otherwise, if it is presumed to contain asbestos, any removal or work on it will need to be done under controlled conditions – particularly if it is a licensable material, and the cost may be much greater.

In addition, of course, where materials are suspected under a Type 1 survey, the dutyholder will be required to manage these (and incur the additional expense) in the asbestos management plan under regulation 4 of CAWR 2002.

There are situations where a Type 1 survey may be justified:

- the area cannot be sampled whilst occupied (a hospital intensive care unit will be occupied 24 hours a day, seven days a week), or
- the age of the building is such that only a few, low risk asbestos materials are likely to have been used (post 1990, for example) and maintenance is very unlikely to disturb these, or
- there are a number of identical units – 10% of which have been surveyed with samples taken for confirmation (Type 2 survey) – housing units, for example.

In a Type 1 survey, however, there is still a requirement that all areas should be accessed as far as is reasonably practicable. In each case the condition of the materials should be assessed.

## Type 2 – standard sampling, identification and assessment survey

This is a full sampling survey and is the principal type expected by the HSE for compliance with regulation 4 of CAWR 2002. The standard of access and inspection is exactly the same as for a Type 1 survey, but now the ACMs found are sampled to confirm the presence or absence of asbestos.

Where a particular item – ceiling tiles or floor tiles, for example – are found throughout a building, it is acceptable to take one or two samples and then "strongly presume" that the other incidences, visually identical to the sampled material, are the same composition. This decision would apply only to homogeneous materials, of course.

Local information about the original construction, extension or any refurbishment of the building may be helpful in making such a decision. In the report, these "strongly presumed" materials will be cross-referred to the original analysed sample. (This "strong presumption" does not, however, make this a Type 1 survey.)

It is usual to carry out sampling and assessment at the same time as the survey inspection but it may be desirable to defer the sampling until the building is unoccupied or after a normal Type 1 survey. In any case, the later sampling allows the sampling team to make a further check that all the asbestos materials have been located by the previous surveyor(s).

Some clients may wish to defer the sampling until later. This may be either for cost reasons or in order to complete the preliminary Type 1 surveys of a large number of sites and buildings, before returning to collect the samples for confirmation.

It is quite usual in a Type 2 sampling survey for some suspected ACMs to be inaccessible for reasons discussed above. In these cases, the ACM should be reported as "presumed" or "strongly presumed" but the material and condition risk assessment should still be carried out.

## Type 3 – Full access sampling and identification survey

This is the appropriate survey prior to any major disturbance of the fabric as part of refurbishment or demolition. It requires access to all areas, including parts of the structure or voids not accessed under a Type 1 or Type 2 survey, and is sometimes referred to as an intrusive or invasive inspection. In particular, it will require inspection of sandwich partitions, inside ducts or risers, or behind cladding where asbestos panels or ACMs are sometimes known to have been located.

Because these surveys will probably require significant disturbance of the building structure, it is important for the surveyor to have:

- adequate PPE and RPE
- equipment for cleaning up any debris released (eg HEPA Type H vacuum cleaner) and personal decontamination to prevent the spread of asbestos

- access equipment, to sample at heights, for example.

It is important for the client to understand that even if a Type 2 survey has been carried out, if refurbishment or demolition is to be undertaken, a Type 3 survey is essential to establish whether there are any other ACMs in the structure. This Type 3 survey would start with the Type 2 survey information and then go on to check for other materials deeper within the structure.

Even where there has been a subsequent phased removal programme after the Type 2 survey, and all the ACMs identified have been removed, a Type 3 survey will still be required to examine the structure in greater depth.

Clients will need to be aware that even where a Type 3 survey has identified ACMs to be removed, subsequent demolition may reveal further ACMs which could not be found even in a Type 3 survey. Examples would include:

- shuttering beneath concrete
- debris deliberately covered over by a concrete slab
- sprayed asbestos hidden by shuttering or other parts of the structure.

Demolition contractors must therefore be alerted to the potential presence of asbestos in the structure and should be ready to hand-pick the debris and remove any ACMs discovered.

# Preparation and Conduct of Surveys

## Pre-site meeting

The pre-site meeting is required to sort out a wide range of issues affecting the conduct of the survey. It may well be that several of these have already been prescribed as part of the tender process, but if not then they must be addressed. This is an important step which, if omitted, may lead to delays and over-runs, misinterpretation of instructions, and possible breakdown of the client-surveyor relationship.

Although not exclusive, the list should include the following points.

### Confirm the scope of the survey – area, sample types and any limits

The surveyor must be clear about the area or areas to be surveyed and any limitations such as areas where access cannot be gained or sample types (floor tiles or textured coatings) not to be sampled. In addition, the client may want to specify that some buildings on a site do or do not need to be inspected, because adequate surveys already exist or because the buildings are very unlikely to contain asbestos. It may be that some buildings require a Type 3 survey and others a Type 2. Where there are a number of identical units, it will be necessary to define what proportion should be Type 2 and the remainder Type 1.

The surveyor may wish to bring to the attention of the client the need to gain access to high levels or confined spaces and hence the need (and cost) of access equipment for this.

## Establish the purpose of the survey, and hence the survey type (MDHS 100)

It may be intrusive to ask the client the purpose of the survey, but it will help to ensure that the information derived is appropriate to their needs. If the survey is to enable demolition or refurbishment, the client may need to be reminded that a Type 2 survey is not adequate. Even where a Type 3 survey is carried out for demolition, the client needs to appreciate that although most asbestos has been found and removed, there may be some still retained within the structure which will only be revealed when the building is being demolished.

The client may wish to insist on a Type 1 non-sampling inspection where the surveyor would recommend a Type 2 sampling survey. The surveyor may need to understand the client's reasons are that it is better to get some information soon (and plan accordingly) rather than to incur the extra cost of sampling and analysis at this stage.

## Schedule of the site work and reporting deadlines

It is clearly necessary to establish a timescale for the survey work and the reporting deadlines. Surveyors must, however, be aware that time pressures (either from the client or their own management) will lead to ACMs being missed or errors being made in the paperwork. If the time pressure is being exerted by the client, it will be necessary to explain the time needed for surveying, analysis and report production.

Where the client has a large number of premises or sites to be inspected it is possible to produce some kind of ranking to determine the priority for surveying. Factors to be taken into account would include:

• the age of the premise
• availability of previous information on the asbestos present
• number of occupants likely to be at risk

- activities which enhance the risk to the occupants
- any refurbishment projects planned.

Very often, surveyors will have rough rules of thumb to estimate the time needed on site for a survey, but these will be greatly dependent on the property type (domestic, office, educational, hospital, utility, heavy industry, etc).

## Access to the site areas and accompanying personnel

The client will need to arrange site access and, in some cases, the surveyors will need to submit details of their personnel on site for clearance by the client's security agency. Surveyors may need to be able to provide some kind of proof of identity on arriving at site, as authorisation or as a security check.

The occupants of the premises to be surveyed must be notified, either by the client or the surveyor, of the date and times of the inspection. It may be necessary in some or all areas (for security or safety reasons) to require the surveyors to be accompanied by the client's representative.

The client will need to indicate whether keys to any locked areas are available and how they can be obtained.

## Site safety matters

Site safety will be discussed in more detail below but the pre-survey site meeting is the ideal point for these matters to be discussed. In some cases, surveyors may need special training in order to access certain areas because of the safety hazards and relevant training will need to be provided.

## Availability of site plans and previous surveys

Again, to be discussed in more detail below, now is the time for this to be raised.

83

## Sampling protocols and exclusions (if any)

Sampling procedures will be discussed in more detail in chapter 8 but, again, it is essential that the client and surveyor agree on sampling frequencies or any exclusions.

## Reporting format, including recommendations for remedial work

This is the opportunity for the client and surveyor to agree on how the results should be recorded and formatted, how many copies of a report to be supplied, whether in electronic database or hard copy form, whether pictures can or should be included. The client may specify how far the surveyor should make recommendations about remedial work where the condition of the ACM is judged to be moderate or poor.

## Procedures to be followed where damaged ACMs are found

It will be normal to notify the client when damaged ACMs are found. The communication procedures should be clearly set out, with contact names and telephone numbers, times when available. The surveyor needs to be clear about who can or should be told of the damaged ACM and when, presumably as quickly as possible. Surveyors should be aware that it is the client's responsibility to notify the occupants of their site and that the surveyor should not cause unnecessary alarm among those in the immediate area. In the vast majority of cases, asbestos debris, which is not being disturbed, even by mild air movement, will not give rise to any measurable airborne fibre concentrations. Problems will only occur where asbestos or debris is being physically disturbed.

The surveyor, however, has a duty of care to ensure that people in the immediate vicinity are not exposed to asbestos unnecessarily, and if the surveyor judges that asbestos is being disturbed, then they should take all reasonable actions to try and halt the disturbance and exposure.

In some cases, it will be appropriate to undertake some (undisturbed) air sampling to establish what levels of airborne fibres are present in the immediate area. Invariably, if the asbestos is not being disturbed and there is minimal activity, the fibre concentrations will be below the normal limit of detection (0.01 f/ml). The sampling is, however, necessary to be able to provide the information as some kind of reassurance.

When notifying the client of damaged asbestos or debris, the surveyor should, wherever possible, be prepared to offer some advice and assistance on what is needed to rectify the situation. In many cases, straightforward isolation of the area, preventing access by unauthorised persons, is the most effective means of preventing exposure for the time being. A knee-jerk resort to expensive asbestos removal is not necessarily the most appropriate short-term action.

# Previous surveys, plans and local information

It will be extremely helpful if the client can supply plans of the building, either "as built" with the architect's specification, which is unlikely in most cases of buildings from the 1950s or 1960s, for example. Otherwise, plans as existing, whether or not they have been amended to allow for any extensions or refurbishment will be helpful. Copies of the plans will be needed to mark up asbestos materials located and sampled and if no plans are available, then the surveyor will need to agree with the client what level of accuracy is needed for the plans. In some cases, CAD plans may be appropriate and the surveyor will need to take this into account.

It will be increasingly common to find buildings that have been previously surveyed. The client may require them to be re-surveyed for ACMs, either because they appreciate the inadequacies of the original surveys or they need now to refurbish or demolish the building.

It should be understood that before the introduction of MDHS 100 and the advent of accreditation of surveyors (via accredited inspection bodies), the quality and completeness of asbestos surveys before 2000 could be dubious. Many older surveys from recognised and established asbestos consultancies should, however, be reasonably reliable. One of the driving forces for the production of MDHS 100 by the HSE was the poor quality of survey information perceived by HSE inspectors in the field.

Surveyors should also be ready to use (as part of a walk-through before the main survey work) the local knowledge of people who were or have been involved in the construction, refurbishment and maintenance of the premises. These would include:

- maintenance or service engineers
- security personnel
- estates management departments
- caretakers or premises managers.

All of these people will be invaluable in gaining access to isolated areas, with their knowledge of the structure (including underground service ducts), the history and the uses of the buildings, dates of any major extensions and refurbishment. Their information, particularly dates, will be very helpful, but any comments on asbestos materials and their presence or absence should be treated with respectful caution, unless the informant is clearly well-qualified in this area. The information may be misleading (or even plain wrong!) and it should be verified by the inspection. It is of course, possible, that old surveys and drawings will have been squirreled away by older staff, unbeknown to higher levels of management. When these resurface, they can be an invaluable source of information (but must of course be verified).

# Site safety matters and risk assessments

The survey activity itself will involve a number of hazards. It is vital that all of these are properly identified and assessed to determine the appropriate measures to be taken to ensure the safety of all concerned, surveyors as well as the normal occupants of the site. The initial identification of the hazards will be a matter for the surveyor, but in some cases, the client will need to bring specific information on their site hazards to the attention of the surveyors.

The risk assessments will need to be carried out by a competent person but in any case, the surveyor should have adequate training in general safety matters as part of their training. As a general kit of safety equipment, the surveyors should always have available:

- hard hats (bump caps)

- safety boots or shoes
- high visibility jackets or waistcoats
- hearing protection (disposable ear plug type)
- goggles or safety glasses.

The most common hazards to be encountered by surveyors include the following.

## Unsafe structures

Where surveyors need to access a derelict building, it will be essential to obtain a structural survey from a qualified structural engineer to ensure that the building is safe to enter and work in. If the area is highly contaminated with asbestos (because of storm damage, for example) it will be necessary to ensure that the structural engineer can enter and leave the area with the appropriate protective equipment and decontamination procedures.

## Working at heights, including fragile or unguarded roofs

This is one of the most common problems for a surveyor, to gain access to ceiling tiles, coating on beams, inspection of roofs and high-level pipework. In some cases, access can be gained with a ladder but if it is above 2 m, then a suitable platform (mobile tower) or cherry picker will be needed. New regulations on working at height will come into effect in the summer of 2004.

Asbestos cement roofs are notoriously fragile and surveyors must not stand on unsupported sheets. Crawl boards or similar must be used.

## Enclosed or confined spaces

If the surveyor needs to enter a confined space, a suitable and sufficient risk assessment must be undertaken. The Confined Spaces Regulations 1996 apply here. It is extremely important to recognise that the definition of a "confined space" covers a wide range of situations and is mostly governed by the use of the area and any chemicals or gases likely to be found or used there. The areas likely to be accessed which could be classed as a "confined space" include:

- underground service ducts
- undercrofts
- inspection pits
- tank rooms (eg for oil or compressed gases).

Access to all these areas may require some kind of checks of air quality for toxic gases or oxygen deficiency. There are many suitable portable detectors available for these checks but they should be calibrated and used by a competent person able to interpret the results.

## Electrical hazards

Surveyors should not normally be disturbing any areas where live electrical installations are to be found unless there is an extremely low risk of contacting live electric cables. If access is needed inside equipment or switchgear, then this must only be gained under the supervision of a qualified competent electrician who can isolate the equipment and make it safe.

Particular situations to be checked include access into

- ceiling voids with metal grids and where there may be frayed cables
- electric storage heaters
- lighting units
- switch gear
- furnaces and ovens where the structure needs to be disturbed.

This restriction should also apply on a supposedly derelict site where it would appear that there is no live power to the site. It would also include a restriction on disturbing 3-phase power cables entering a building: these are sometimes found wrapped with a chrysotile cloth and a bitumen paint.

If plaster walls or partitions need to be disturbed in a Type 3 survey, then a cable detector must be used.

# Chemical hazards

On chemical plant sites (or, indeed, any site where chemicals are used), it will be vital for the surveyors to be aware of the chemical hazards present. The risk assessment will have to include an identification of the chemicals and locations, and the appropriate PPE for the surveyors. It is difficult to provide comprehensive guidance here, but this area is clearly a matter of joint responsibility for both client and surveyor.

# Microbiological hazards

These are not always immediately obvious, but include the following.

### Weil's disease (Leptospirosis)

This is highly dangerous. Infection is caused by contact with the agent from rats' urine in water, eg from a flooded basement in a derelict building. The contact need only be quite brief. The disease begins with flu-like symptoms and can be fatal if not treated in time.

### Legionnaires' disease (Legionellosis)

From building water systems without proper treatment or controls, particularly mists from spray systems, showers or air-conditioning plant. Although potentially fatal, of course, it mostly affects the elderly or infirm, or people with reduced or impaired immune systems. It is not infectious from one person to another, however.

### Aids/Hepatitis B

This is possibly the most significant problem, especially where surveyors are visiting derelict premises or housing estates where drugs or drug-related crime is known to be a problem. Discarded infected syringes may be found from drug users, sometimes stored (and not necessarily for later retrieval) in places where it seems have been chosen deliberately to cause maximum danger to the unwary. For example they have both been found under banister rails, above door frames, in cracks in brickwork, etc. Surveyors must be extremely careful of their safety in these premises.

## Anthrax

Anthrax is known to have been a problem in very old plasters (up to the 1930s) reinforced with horsehair, potentially infected with anthrax spores. The spores are viable for many decades and great care should be taken when sampling these materials. As there are two routes of infection, cutaneous and respiratory, both PPE (including gloves) and RPE should be worn. If at all possible, avoid disturbing these materials.

Analysis and detection of anthrax in materials is a specialist activity. For information and analysis, contact the Health Protection Agency (formerly Public Health Laboratory Service (PHLS)) at http://www.hpa.org.uk. Alternatively, contact a veterinary analytical laboratory at http://www.defra.gov.uk/corporate/vla/aboutus/locations.htm.

# Noise

Noise is not normally a significant problem in a survey, except where surveyors need to work in a live boiler house or industrial plant areas, such as power stations. Boiler fans and pumps may be extremely noisy, and it is quite simple for the surveyor to be provided with disposable hearing protectors. Disposable foam ear plugs are more suitable than ear muffs. Specialist advice should be obtained.

# Lone working on isolated sites

It is normal practice for surveyors to work in teams of two for a variety of reasons. One reason is to provide security when working on isolated or unoccupied sites. In every case, the surveyors should have made it clear to their office management or supervisor or to the site management the times they expect to be on site (start and finish) and approximate locations. They must be provided with mobile telephones, two-way radios, pagers or similar systems for adequate communication in emergency. They may need to arrange to ring into the office at specified intervals to confirm that all is well.

# Heat stress

This is not often a problem but should be considered when working in live plant rooms or in plants where heat-generation is a major factor. In particular, consider problems with access at high levels where hot air may collect, creating a temperature gradient not immediately obvious from ground level. Hot surfaces create a serious potential for burns on skin contact.

## Entry into and exit from contaminated areas

It is not unusual to find that a plant room or other area is heavily contaminated with asbestos debris on the floor. There is then a serious risk of surveyors spreading the debris outside the area when leaving. They need to assess the condition visually before entering the area to ensure they can leave safely without spreading asbestos outside. Procedures are described in chapter 8.

## Suspended ceilings

Examination in suspended ceilings is essential, even though the ceiling tiles are apparently not asbestos. However, caution is needed in entering the void as disturbing the tiles may dislodge debris on the topside of the new ceiling from damage to an original ceiling still in place. A little thought needs to be given as to what may be reasonably expected above the ceiling and how access can be gained safely: see also pp 115–117 in chapter 8 below.

# Systematic approach to the inspection

As any surveyor of experience will appreciate, a systematic structured approach to the survey inspection is absolutely vital to ensure that the inspection is conducted thoroughly and that, so far as is reasonably practicable, all ACMs are identified in the survey. It is extremely easy to come across something unusual or exceptional and to be diverted and then miss something obvious which should have been picked up.

The way to overcome this is to use some kind of structured approach, looking at the building elements in a set sequence, perhaps using a checklist. The inspection should start outside the building, to obtain a view of the age of the building and hence the likely asbestos materials to be found, and also to inspect the exterior for asbestos materials.

The inspection should include the following elements:

- ceilings and ceiling voids
- exterior walls
- interior walls
- risers
- floors and floor ducts
- heating systems
- ventilation systems
- other fixtures and fittings.

# Recording of data

The eventual report to the client may also determine the way in which data is recorded. Data may be collected either electronically or on paper. In some cases, the client may require electronic recording for download to a mainframe or network system, particularly where they have a software system already installed for recording the data and risk assessments. A number of systems have been used. The surveyor should ensure that the software is appropriate and useable for field use and that the hardware is also sufficiently robust for site work.

The software should be economical for data entry. Repetitious entries of building reference, floor and room number for each item will be extremely tiresome and will increase the risk of errors in data transcription. It should be possible to check the accuracy of the data entered before returning to site to download the data.

There are several commercial databases of varying complexity and cost. For a small site a workable Microsoft Access™ database is cheap and simple to construct but for a multi-site organisation with many buildings under the day-to-day control of many people, it is probably worth using a more elaborate (and more expensive) system.

The final register determines the information to be collected. The surveyor must be clear about the structure of the data. If the system requires an assessment of "degree of damage" or "accessibility" the surveyor should be clear how the client expects these parameters to be evaluated. It may well be left to the surveyor's professional judgment but it is worth asking the question. If several surveyors are involved in the same site or project, there needs to be a degree of consistency between them.

If the MDHS 100/HSG 227 materials risk assessment and management prioritisation scoring systems are to be used, it will be necessary to establish which data items will be collected by the surveyor and which (if any) is to be supplied by the client.

# Remediation options

The final report will probably include some recommendations for repairs and remedial works. It is worth agreeing with the client that any recommendations made are not binding on the client, of course, providing that adequate control of the ACM prevents exposure of persons in this area. The surveyor must remember that the client has his own agenda and future plans for the building will determine the appropriate short to medium term management actions.

The range of appropriate remedial actions will include the following:

*   label ACMs in good condition and keep under observation (reassessment)
*   minor repairs (paint seal or encapsulate), then label and keep under observation
*   enclose asbestos in good condition with a rigid covering (metal cladding, wood panels, etc) to improve protection
*   clear any debris, repair and seal/encapsulate, label and keep under observation
*   remove ACM which is damaged or has deteriorated beyond economic repair or which is subject to major refurbishment or demolition.

Removal of the ACM would be strictly required only where:

*   the material is beyond economic repair
*   the ACM is vulnerable to further damage
*   a change of use makes it more vulnerable to damage
*   refurbishment or demolition is proposed.

Otherwise, the HSE's view is that it is safer to seal the ACM and leave it undisturbed. Removal (and disposal) incurs great costs and leaves risks of low-level exposure of airborne asbestos fibres within an occupied building for some while after the removal. In addition, there may be short-term problems with providing sufficient disposal site capacity if all the asbestos materials were to be removed within the next year or so – as well as the likely short-fall in capacity in the asbestos removal industry.

The question of labelling ACMs will be raised again in chapter 12 on Asbestos Management Plans.

# Air sampling

Although not essential in every case, air sampling may be appropriate in three specific cases:

1. Static samples after the survey work is completed to demonstrate the area has not been contaminated by the sampling process. This would be required only where the site is of a sensitive nature and the information is required really for public relations purposes.
2. Static samples where significant debris is located in an area which would appear normally to be accessed from time to time at least. As long as this has not been disturbed at the time, however, it is very unlikely to show any significant levels of airborne fibres.
3. Personal samples taken on the surveyors while sampling to demonstrate that they have not been exposed to significant amounts of airborne asbestos and that their exposure does not exceed the action level. These results would still need to go into their personal exposure records.

    It would not be necessary to do such personal monitoring on a frequent basis. Initially, a frequency of monthly would be sensible. Once the data is shown to be giving very low levels or levels below the limit of detection, the frequency can be reduced to quarterly, for example.

Results from the static samples (1) and (2) will be provided for the client and samples therefore will need to be taken and analysed by a laboratory accredited by UKAS (regulation 19 of the CAWR 2002). If the personal samples (3) are solely for the surveyor's own organisation (and are taken by members of the organisation), accreditation is not required but that surveyor's organisation must have an appropriate quality management system which meets the requirements of ISO 17025.

# Sampling Techniques and Strategies

Sampling is critical to the usefulness of the survey results. There are a number of specific practical requirements:

- the sample must be representative of the material, bearing in mind it may not be homogeneous, and, as a corollary ....
- it must not be cross-contaminated, especially if the material is nominally asbestos-free
- the sample size must be sufficient to enable the analyst to analyse the sample and report the correct types of asbestos present (or absent)
- sample size must be sufficient to be able to detect "traces" of asbestos if present
- The sample documentation must be traceable to the material and sample point.

For a Type 2 survey, the sampled materials should be left intact and serviceable so far as is practicable, and the client's guidance should be sought if inevitable damage is going to occur. This is a matter for the pre-survey meeting. There is a fine balance to be made between taking sufficient sample for the analysis and causing excessive damage to the fabric and decorations. For Type 2 surveys, therefore, sampling points should be as discreet as possible.

There is no excuse for a Type 3 survey, however, for simply attacking or vandalising the materials and leaving the area as a mess. Even if the building is not currently occupied, the area will inevitably need to be accessed by others later on. Any debris caused by the sampling must be cleaned up.

# MDHS 100

The sampling of materials is discussed in both MDHS 77 and MDHS 100. This is an interesting overlap, but most of the detail is given in MDHS 100.

Surveyors tend to carry a kit of general tools with them, including a mixture of specific sampling items. The kit will include a mix of screwdrivers (flat and cross-head) in order to access various panels and covers, possibly battery-powered if a number of grilles or panels need to be removed. Some essential items are listed below.

## *Torch (rechargeable or with spare batteries)*

This is an absolute necessity. A good quality torch, not too heavy, but focusing (eg Mag-lite® type), but preferably stable when put down to prevent it rolling off a platform.

## *Camera (digital or conventional silver halide film type)*

Digital cameras are now so cheap, of such good quality, so convenient, versatile and powerful that for this purpose an old silver halide film type seems entirely redundant. Digital images can, of course, be checked and retaken immediately if not satisfactory. Even one-hour processing cannot compete with the ease of downloading and manipulating digital images, and photographs will still have to be scanned if they are to be incorporated into a database.

The only proviso is that some measure of security needs to be made if digital images are to be presented as evidence to be presented in a dispute or in a court of law, because of the ease of manipulating digital images. (Some film processors will now also produce digital images on a CD-ROM or on an internet site, possibly at very small extra cost.)

The recommended type of digital camera should ideally have a minimum of two mega-pixels to provide adequate resolution, with zoom lens, auto focus and integral flash. A suitable camera will cost less than £100.

Picture sizes larger than 4 or 5 mega-pixels are really not justified: the file size will be excessive. The standard graphics file type now is .jpg. This provides file sizes very much smaller than the old .bmp or .tif types. If necessary, files should be converted with a suitable graphics software programme and saved as .jpg files for easy manipulation.

## Step-ladders

Good quality stepladders are invariably needed for access. They should be stable and capable of providing a solid work platform for sampling at high level. Lightweight aluminium steps are adequate if they are of industrial (not domestic) grade.

## Wet-wipes

These are universally useful for cleaning up small amounts of debris, cleaning sampling tools and personal decontamination after sampling.

## Sample labels

Many survey organisations have their own pre-printed sample labels, which they will use to mark each sample point. The label will have the organisation name and telephone number, and space for a sample reference number. The purpose of the label is to indicate that a sample has been taken and to enable someone else to ring up the surveyor for information about that sample. Obviously, the label does not indicate whether the material contains asbestos or not.

Labelling of sample points in normally occupied areas may not be acceptable to the client and this will need to be discussed.

# Safety equipment – PPE and RPE

## General PPE

Surveyors will need to make suitable safety risk assessments (see chapter 7) for non-asbestos hazards.

## Overalls

Disposable Tyvek® overalls of the type used by asbestos removal contractors are quite suitable. Tyvek® is a registered trademark of the Du Pont company. The material is based on high-density polyethylene (HDPE) fibres. This is the single-piece hooded type with elasticated wrist and ankles.

The type used by the contractors is of a better standard than is required by surveyors but the important property is the dust penetration resistance. Laundry of used overalls would have to be done with specialist facilities and is therefore not a realistic option for surveyors.

For sampling it is normally quite acceptable for the overalls to be worn over other clothing. Disposable overalls should be disposed of as asbestos waste after a sampling session. If sampling has to be carried out in a number of locations in a single day, the surveyor must be sure that no asbestos contamination is being spread throughout the site.

When removing overalls, turn them inside out as they are removed to trap any surface dust and immediately place them in the polythene bag in which they were supplied. Always remove RPE after PPE.

## Disposable overshoes

Protective overshoes in Tyvek® are also available. These must be worn where there is clear evidence of debris and must be removed and disposed of as asbestos waste when leaving the area. (If the amount of debris is gross, the surveyor should not consider entering the area unless adequate procedures are in place (possibly including an airlock) for entering and exiting the area without spreading asbestos outside the area.)

## Respiratory protective equipment

The RPE used is of three main types:

* disposable filtering face piece
* half mask (orinasal) filtering or
* full face filtering masks.

The disposable type should comply with the standard in BS EN 149. The standard specifies filtration grades of P1, P2 and P3, in increasing filtration efficiency. P1 is suitable for coarse non-toxic dusts, while P3 is suitable for fine toxic dusts. P3 grade should be used for *all* asbestos sampling activities.

The disposable types will be labelled FFP3 and the filters for the half mask or full-face mask type will be labelled P3.

Users of RPE for asbestos must have passed a satisfactory face-fit test (preferably quantitative) when the RPE is first supplied and must hold a face fit certificate for each type of RPE used, including disposable types. It is not normally necessary to repeat the face-fit test unless the subject has changed weight significantly or undergone major dental surgery, for example. Where the performance of the RPE depends on achieving a seal, a fit test cannot be carried out for RPE wearers with beards or with stubble.

The choice of RPE for each situation will be determined by the risk of exposure. Surveyors will need to have generic risk assessments for each situation but as a general guide, the following RPE should be used for various sampling activities.

| *Respirator type* | *Materials to be sampled* |
|---|---|
| Disposable | Cement |
| | Rope or textiles |
| | Collecting AIB debris |
| Half mask | Insulating board |
| | Mill board |
| | Textured coatings |
| | Collecting insulation debris |
| Full-face mask | Pipe insulation |
| | Spray coatings |

Ideally, however, surveyors should be using the best RPE to reduce exposure to asbestos as far as is reasonably practicable. For more details refer to the example risk assessments in HSE's IND(G) 288.

For sampling materials that are fully bonded, such as floor tiles, gaskets or roofing felt, surveyors will need to make their own risk assessments and decide what (if any) RPE is required.

The presence of debris or materials in poor condition will clearly indicate a need for wearing RPE of a higher grade than otherwise required.

RPE can be obtained from a number of specialist suppliers and distributors and, in the case of the larger organisations, they can also perform the quantitative fit test referred to above. Preferably choose a distributor who supplies masks from a range of manufacturers. It is far better to have a mask which the wearer feels comfortable and happy with, as well as giving the correct degree of protection.

## Gloves

Some surveyors like to use disposable latex gloves for protection. When removing these, clean them with a wet-wipe and then peel them off so they are inside out. Dispose of them as asbestos waste.

## HEPA Type H vacuum cleaner (BS 5415)

Surveyors may need access to a HEPA Type H vacuum cleaner to clean up debris. In most cases, small amounts of debris can be cleaned up with wet wipes but in extreme cases, the vacuum cleaner will be needed. This clearly must be of the appropriate type and must be tested at six-monthly intervals. (Under no circumstances, of course, can an ordinary domestic vacuum cleaner be used for asbestos.)

## Area preparation

Ideally, sampling should only be undertaken when an area is unoccupied by the normal occupants or other members of the general public. Since the surveyors will usually be wearing PPE and RPE, other occupants will understandably be rather nervous. The surveyors may need to arrange for sampling access when the area is not occupied or in use or to exclude the occupants temporarily.

It is normal to try to prevent access while samples are being taken by putting up notices ("Sampling in progress" for example – avoiding the word "asbestos") and/or the use of barrier tape to discourage people from entering.

This is very likely to be a sensitive issue for occupants and surveyors need to have discussed this with their client.

# Entry into contaminated areas

When entering an area such as a boiler or plant room where there is a possibility of asbestos debris, plans must be made for safe entry and exit to these areas, and to prevent the spread of asbestos outside the area. Surveyors should consider very carefully the need to enter any contaminated area at all.

Typical locations include:

- plant rooms or boiler rooms with asbestos insulation
- ceiling voids
- floor ducts
- undercroft
- riser ducts.

A preliminary inspection at the entrance should readily show how clean the area is. If there is evidence of debris, the following procedures should be adopted:

(i) At the entrance, while still in a "clean" area, put on disposable overall, disposable overshoes and RPE.

(ii) Lay a clean sheet of polythene on the floor at the entrance, and then enter the area with sampling kit and equipment.

When the inspection and sampling is complete, leave the area with the following procedures:

(i) Take all kit and equipment to the entrance, wipe it off if necessary with a wet-wipe and place it on the polythene sheet.

(ii) Remove overshoes and then stand on the clean polythene sheet – dispose of overshoes in waste bag.

(iii) Remove overalls and dispose of them in the waste bag.

(iv) Wipe hands and respirator with wet-wipes.

(v) Withdraw outside the area, remove the equipment and waste bag, and clean the polythene sheet with wet-wipe.

(vi) Peel off disposable latex gloves (if used) and dispose of as asbestos waste.

(vii) Remove RPE and store.

In the very worst situations, where there is known to be substantial debris, surveyors should consider alternatives before entering the area. If it is necessary to enter the area to inspect it, perhaps collect a sample or two of debris and take photographs, it may be necessary to use a licensed asbestos removal contractor to construct a three-stage airlock at the entry point. The area will need to be treated as a respirator zone and entry should be restricted to competent trained persons. Normal clothing in this case should not be worn under protective overalls. Decontamination procedures may need to be adopted when exiting from this area, and a suitable hygiene unit will be needed.

**Fig. 8.1** Badly damaged pipe insulation in a ceiling void

Maintenance engineers have used this walkway over the years and completely destroyed the insulation. This area must be isolated until a full clean up of the whole ceiling void can be carried out.

# Sampling pipe insulation

Pipe insulation is the least uniform of all the materials likely to be sampled, both from top to bottom and along the length of the pipe. The standard sampler is the core borer, which needs to be long enough to reach the bottom layer of the insulation at the pipe surface. Present designs are based on the old traditional laboratory cork borer which can be perfectly adequate and is still sometimes used. The core diameter is usually about 12–25 mm diameter but may be thinner if it is necessary to get through a layer of chicken wire sometimes found between layers of insulation.

A very good version, originally designed by Shutler Associates, is now produced and marketed by JS Holdings. For information, contact enquiries@jsholdings.co.uk. This set can be supplied with two different widths of corers.

**Fig 8.2** Examples of two types of core samplers

JS Holdings version is on the right.

Usually the metal from which the samplers are made is quite soft and it will be found necessary to sharpen the corers regularly. The standard type of laboratory cork borer sharpener is quite satisfactory.

If the insulation has a hard-set plaster or cement finish, this may be accessed by using a serrated core tool to saw through the outer case. Alternatively, it may be possible to hand drill with a spade bit and "shadow vacuum" to access the insulation below. Where the insulation is clad with heavy gauge aluminium, this technique cannot be used. Here it will be necessary to access the insulation at the end where the folded flaps of the aluminium can be opened carefully to reveal the insulation.

For this activity, full RPE and PPE must be worn in all cases, whether the sampling is internal or in the open air.

The recognised sampling procedure is set out below.

## Preparation of the sampling point

Select a sampling point at the lowest convenient point on the pipe and preferably not above eye level. (If the sampling point is above eye level, goggles or a full-face mask must be worn for eye protection.) Place a clean sheet of polythene below the sample point to collect any debris that may be released. Prepare the sample point by wrapping tape completely around the circumference of the pipe, to hold it in place in case the sampling disturbs the bulk of the insulation. This is particularly important where the insulation is in less than perfect condition; sometimes a bit of force is needed to penetrate the outer casing of the insulation.

The preferred type of tape is duct tape, preferably 75mm wide; the adhesion of aluminium foil tape is not always good on some kinds of pipe work, such as soft calico or cloth outer layers, and certainly not on wet surfaces.

Ideally, the insulation should be injected with fibre suppressant (Astrip® works well but a home-made mixture of glycerol, washing up liquid and water is equally satisfactory). This can be injected with a low-pressure garden spray, for example, but it requires the use of a needle with sufficient length to reach the surface of the pipe.

The sample should be taken from the top or from the side of the pipe to minimise the risk of debris falling out of the sample point.

## Preparation of the sampling tool

Check that the core sampler is clean. It should have been cleaned after the previous sample. If necessary, clean it inside and out with wet-wipes before use. Cross-contamination of samples must be prevented.

Insert a wet-wipe in the end of the sampler but don't push it right down to the end of the sampler. Leave a gap. Wrap another wet-wipe around the outside of the sampler and hold this so that it seals the point of entry. The wet-wipes are to prevent the release of dust (if the wetting is not effective or has not been used) from the sample point and from the core sampler and eventually to clean the sampler as well.

## Taking the sample

Carefully insert the core sampler into the insulation and twist/push it fully down to the surface of the pipe. It is particularly important to collect all the layers of insulation. When removing the sampler, place the outer wet-wipe over the end to prevent the spread of any dust from the sampler. Place the end of the sampler into a self-seal polythene sample bag. Wipe the outside of the sampler with the wet-wipe and place it in the sample bag. Using a plunger push the inner wet-wipe and sample into the bag. Both wet-wipes should be included in the sample bag.

Alternatively, cap the sampler on both ends and place the sampler and sample into the bag. (The core sampler will be cleaned by the laboratory and later returned to the surveyor.)

If a layer of chicken wire is encountered in the pipe insulation, it may be necessary to take the sample in two stages, and cut the chicken wire with side cutters to get through to the lower layer(s). In such a case, the two parts of the sample can be combined in the same sample bag and it is not necessary to report the compositions of the two separate layers.

## Sealing the sample point

The sample point now needs to be made good by backfilling with an inert filler. Combustible materials such as tissues must not be used and handling MMMF is undesirable since it is rated as a Class 2 carcinogen (suspected human carcinogen). The preferred solution is to use a proprietary material such as Polyfilla®, which can be conveniently dispensed from a tube. Cover the sample point neatly with tape and a sample label to indicate that a sample has been taken.

## Securing the sample

The sample bag must be securely sealed and each sample individually double-bagged in a similar bag. Again, this is important to prevent cross-contamination of the samples.

# Sampling spray coatings

Spray coatings are likely to be homogeneous in composition. However, although HMSO's *Asbestos Materials in Buildings* referred to layered coatings – crocidolite or amosite with an over-coating of chrysotile – in practice this is rarely seen. The major problem is the danger of disturbing the very soft and friable material and releasing fibres into the atmosphere. Every precaution must be taken to prevent the release and spread of debris. It may be possible to inject fibre suppressant as before, but this should be done with great care.

A core sampler can be used if the coating is sealed or encapsulated and in good condition. If there is debris which can easily be removed and is clearly the same material, then it is acceptable to simply collect the material with a pair of tweezers and place into the sample bag.

If the coating is encapsulated with a calico cloth and flexible sealant, the cloth can be carefully cut with a sharp knife or scalpel and then the coating sampled with the core sampler as above (or even with a pair of tweezers). However, if the coating is not sealed in any way, great care must be taken to prevent any damage and spread of debris.

Overspray on adjacent surfaces is found in many cases. This need not be sampled but must be noted on the condition assessment and survey report.

# Sampling insulating board

If the board is damaged it may be possible to remove a suitable piece for analysis. Unfortunately, life is rarely that simple, and it may require some damage to extract a suitable sample, which potentially releases debris and airborne fibres. Ideally the board should be wetted with a spray before sampling to reduce the release of airborne fibres. Sealed or painted boards obviously resist the use of wetting sprays unless the unsealed (back) surface can be accessed.

The two main methods of removing a sample are:

(a)  A sharp bladed scraper or chisel or similar to remove a flake at a corner of the panel.
(b)  A pair of flat-jawed pliers (as used by glaziers) to remove a suitable sized piece; as an alternative, ordinary serrated-jaw pliers can be used if the serrations are protected with a tissue or wet-wipe to prevent contamination.

In both cases, debris will be released so the area must be protected with a polythene sheet beneath the sampling point, RPE and PPE must be worn. Again, in both cases, the use of a wet-wipe around the board will help to prevent the spread of any debris.

The sample size needed for analysis ideally should be about 2 cm² as a minimum. The main asbestos components will be obvious and easy to find in the sample but there may be small traces of other asbestos types present also, so (if possible) a slightly larger sample may be desirable.

# Sampling bonded materials, cement, floor tiles and gaskets

## Cement sheet and pipe

Cement sheet or pipe is very hard and sampling usually poses little risk of fibre release. The trickiest problem is to break a piece off a sheet corner, for example, with a pair of flat-jawed pliers or even mole grips provided the jaws are protected with wet-wipes.

Sampling a pipe is probably easiest at a sleeve or collar joint where it may be possible to remove a sample with a very sharp knife or small hacksaw blade. When using a hacksaw blade the material must be covered with a wet-wipe to catch any dust released and any debris must be cleared up, of course. If the pipe is "live" and likely to remain so, it would be quite justifiable (and probably better) to presume it contains asbestos, and avoid the sampling problem altogether.

The sample size required is preferably about 2 cm², but in difficult situations the analyst may have to settle for rather less, as otherwise the damage may be excessive.

## Thermoplastic floor tiles, gaskets or roofing felt

A sharp knife or scalpel is adequate, preferably taking a sample in a discreet location, where sampling will not damage the integrity and functioning of the material.

Sample size required should be about 2 cm², but for partially concealed materials such as gaskets or damp-proof course (DPC) it may be difficult to get that much. A gasket will be of high asbestos content so a smaller sample may be permitted

## Rope seals or textiles

These can simply be cut carefully with a sharp knife after wetting the material to suppress fibre release. A small sample about 1 cm² is more than adequate, as these will be homogeneous and of high asbestos content.

## Sampling textured coatings

Textured coatings pose serious problems, both for the surveyor and the analyst. It is well recognised that the reliability of analysis by polarised light microscopy is particularly poor and collecting sufficient sample without causing unsightly damage is awkward.

Textured coatings are usually sampled with a sharp flat-bladed scraper such as a chisel, directly into the sample bag held underneath the sampling point. It is important, obviously, to get beneath the surface paint layers but not into or below the substrate. The concentration of asbestos is low and not well distributed in the material, so ideally the sample volume needs to be about half a teaspoon, (3–5 ml) which will mean scraping about 10 cm², depending on the thickness of the coating. This naturally means some unsightly damage, which will not be appreciated by the owners or residents. The sample points should be repaired or sealed as far as possible, perhaps with filler or paint.

# Surface dust

A number of techniques are suggested in HSE's MDHS 77. They include the following techniques.

- Micro-vacuuming the surface dust on to an in-line membrane filter and then recovering the dust by dissolution. (Cellulose or glass fibre filters must not be used as they potentially introduce "foreign" fibres.)
- Wiping a smooth non-porous surface with the inside of a polythene sample bag which is then reversed and sealed.
- The dust layer carefully scraped into a suitable container. This is particularly suitable where the dust layer is quite thick.
- Use of adhesive tape or forensic tape (or a membrane filter – not GF or cellulose) to collect the surface dust. Some forensic tapes have water-soluble coatings and the dust is therefore easier to retrieve by washing and drying.

Brushing the surface dust is not permitted because it may generate airborne dust levels and, of course, the brush becomes contaminated.

# Debris

Where there is evident debris the surveyor will need to decide whether it is necessary to take a sample from both the original material and the debris, even though they appear to be the same. This is particularly the case for pipe insulation, spray coatings and insulating board where the debris may have fallen some distance or where the debris has been disturbed and spread.

The recommendation to the client will naturally be that the debris should be cleared up. If the original material, however, can be repaired and encapsulated, then it is important to record the debris as a separate item, because that will remain in the register to be managed and the debris will have been cleared up.

# Sampling frequencies and repetitive areas

The number of samples to be collected is one of the questions where it is difficult (and perhaps undesirable) to lay down fixed rules; an element of discretion will be required from the surveyor. Various sources have quoted specific sampling rates but these must be viewed with caution. Clearly a balance needs to be struck between insufficient samples (and reliance on "presumption") and excessive sampling with unnecessary cost to the surveyor or the client.

One of the earliest recommendations was the original *Asbestos Materials in Buildings*, first published by the Department of the Environment in the early 1980s. (The third and last edition was published in 1991.) Annex 2 included recommendations on sampling frequencies, but, in the case of sampling pipe insulation, these err on the side of caution and will seem to be excessive in some situations. (This protocol was reproduced in *Asbestos and MMMF in Buildings* published by the DETR in 2001.)

MDHS 100 includes recommendations on sampling numbers but rightly it is fairly general in its approach.

## *Repetitive installations*

It is very common to find the same material used throughout areas of a building, particularly items such as:

* ceiling tiles
* floor tiles
* gaskets
* textured coatings
* window boards ("Massal")
* AC roofing sheet
* boiler flues
* riser panels or boxing
* stair nosing.

In such cases, repetitive sampling is wasteful. If the surveyor can ascertain (from building records and/or by inspection) that items in a series of rooms are the same then it is acceptable to take one sample and cross-refer further installations to the first sample with a note that the later examples are "strongly presumed" and not sampled.

Surveyors, however, must be absolutely sure that the repeated materials are indeed the same. For some materials, particularly floor tiles, gaskets and textured coatings, it is much more likely that there will be variations in the times when these were installed, so a distinct note of caution is needed here.

Some general guidelines can be suggested.

## Spray coatings

These are usually fairly consistent throughout a building because they will have been introduced at an early stage in construction of the building. If an extension has been added or major refurbishment has already been carried out it is possible to find examples of asbestos and non-asbestos sprayed coatings together. However, unless these are immediately adjacent, (or the spray coating clearly has a blue colour) it will not be easy to recognise which is which. The architect's specification for the building and the maintenance/refurbishment history of the building should be consulted for information.

Asbestos coatings were sometimes applied with a pre-coating on the substrate of an adhesive layer such as bitumen. This means that when stripping the asbestos it is likely to be extremely difficult to get back to a clean surface and it is possible, therefore, to find evidence of asbestos debris underneath a replacement non-asbestos coating. Unless necessary for a Type 3 survey, this need not be investigated further but the *possibility* of asbestos debris should be highlighted in the survey report.

Because these materials are usually consistent through a building (and if supported by visual examination), two samples at different parts of the structure will be sufficient.

## Thermal insulation

*Asbestos Materials in Buildings* (p13 para 3.2) recommended a very detailed sampling programme for pipe insulation.

In general, one sample should be taken per three metre run of pipe, with particular attention paid to different layers and ... elbows, taps and valves

... For longer pipe runs (over 20 m) one sample per six metres will usually be sufficient. Samples should be taken as a "core" of approximately 5 cm² cross-section, to include all material between the inner and outer surfaces. At least two samples of boiler lagging should be taken on any one unit. Additional samples should be taken from each "patched" area.

For even a moderately complex plant room it is immediately obvious that this could result in unnecessarily large sample numbers. This sampling protocol (in Annex 2) was sometimes included by large organisations (particularly central and local government agencies) in the contract specification for asbestos surveys, perhaps without a full appreciation of the implications.

The sampling strategy will be determined by the purpose of the survey. If the pipe work is due to be stripped, then a couple of samples to demonstrate the presence of asbestos are sufficient; all the insulation will then be stripped as asbestos. For a bank of pipes which all appear to be the same colour and size with no repairs or modifications, it would be reasonable to assume that they were all insulated at the same time with the same material, so one or two samples would suffice.

However, trying to demonstrate that all the pipe insulation is asbestos free (from contamination after a strip) may be more difficult and would require more samples to be taken. (In such a case, the documentary evidence of the building history becomes even more important.)

The number of samples must be left to the discretion of the surveyor, bearing in mind his understanding of the history and the immediate future of the building.

Some areas must be examined.


- It was common to find elbows on pipework insulated with different materials. For example, sectional MMMF insulation may have been used on the straight sections but the elbows insulated with composition asbestos or wound with chrysotile rope.
- Debris under re-insulation of stripped pipe work. It may be necessary to gently remove some of the new insulation to look beneath it, at the pipe surface and at flanges.
- Debris on the walls and floor. It was (and still is) very common to find "snowballs" on the walls where laggers had thrown lumps of the wet insulation around as horseplay, although

smaller lumps will often be found painted over, so any suspicious lumps on the walls should be investigated. Sumps, gullies and awkward areas behind or underneath calorifier or boiler plinths, which would have been difficult to clean, should also be examined.

- Electrical switchgear and cable trays very often are left with debris after poor quality removal of previous insulation. These areas should be examined, if necessary with the assistance of a qualified electrician to isolate equipment for examination.

## Textured coatings

Different coating patterns indicate possibly different materials (or applied at different times) so these should be inspected carefully. Usually one sample per surface (ceiling or wall) will be sufficient and if all the walls in a room are the same then one sample is adequate.

One procedure which many samplers follow is to take five sub-samples, one from each corner and the centre of a surface. These are then combined as a single sample and this procedure improves the likelihood of detecting the asbestos. Unfortunately, this procedure increases the damage to the decorations, of course.

Usually the coating is onto plaster or plasterboard. In rare cases, it may have been coated onto pre-sealed asbestos insulating board which may "contaminate" the sample during the sample collection. If this is apparent, it should be noted, and it would then also be important to collect a separate sample of the substrate.

## Asbestos insulating board

The sheets should be examined very carefully to ensure that all are the same, and, if so, then one sample per room is sufficient. Otherwise, one sample per type is needed. The commonly quoted rate of 1 per 25m$^2$ could be excessive (see MDHS 100).

## AC products

All AC materials (flat sheet, corrugated panels, pipes, tanks and other moulded products) are homogeneous. In older buildings it is reasonable to presume these materials to contain asbestos but it may be excessive to take samples to detect traces of amphibole – in any case, this will not have a large impact on how the material is dealt with. One sample per type of product may be adequate and other samples needed only where the appearance indicates replacement materials have been used.

The dangers of accessing fragile corrugated asbestos cement roofs means that sampling may be limited in any case.

## Floor tiles

The only requirements here are that single samples of each type or colour are needed (about 2 $cm^2$ each sample) and it would be prudent to sample the adhesive as well.

## Apparently non-asbestos materials

Surveyors should be suitably cautious about materials which they would normally recognise as non-asbestos, particularly materials which appear to be MMMF. Some older materials have been seen blended with asbestos (chrysotile and amosite have been seen in separate examples) in ceiling tiles and in loose insulation materials.

The other well-known example is in non-asbestos boards such as Supalux™ or Masterboard™ which are Cape Boards products, widely used as replacements for asbestos insulating boards. Early examples of these or similar boards have been found with small amounts of amosite, perhaps from contamination on the production line, or maybe trial formulations or as a desire to use up old stocks of amosite while moving over to a non-asbestos product.

All the strange mixtures appear in old materials. It would be prudent to sample older materials but if they are evidently new it would be reasonable to presume them to be asbestos free.

However, account must be taken of anything concealed by these materials. It was possible, for example, for asbestos insulating board to be protected with plywood, plasterboard or "Supalux"™.

# Suspended ceilings

For suspended ceilings there are four particular problems:

1.  It has occasionally been found that suspended ceiling tiles (asbestos) have been removed and replaced with equivalent non-asbestos tiles. However, where smoke detectors or sprinkler heads were previously installed a few of the original asbestos tiles may not have been replaced – so now just a few asbestos tiles remain where the majority are asbestos-free. The differences may not always be obvious, particularly if painted. Examination of the unsealed top surfaces, if accessible, may be more illuminating.
2.  Where a suspended ceiling comes below the top of a window in a room with a high ceiling, it is usual to find an upstand, or return, at the edge by the window. Where the original asbestos ceiling tiles in the ceiling have been replaced with non-asbestos tiles the asbestos upstand may still remain. The upstand is most likely to be seen when viewed from within the ceiling void. It may be particularly difficult to sample and it may be necessary to "presume" or "strongly presume" that this contains asbestos.
3.  It is common to find that a new non-asbestos ceiling has been installed beneath the original asbestos tiles. (An example has been seen with three ceilings each below the previous one). New hangers have been inserted through (or attached to) the old ceiling and debris from it can be found on the top of the new tiles (Fig. 8.3).
4.  The top of the ceiling tiles (although not asbestos) may have debris from ACMs in the ceiling void. In particular it is common to find:
    *   damaged asbestos insulating board fire-breaks (where electricians or telecomm engineers have inserted cables, for example)
    *   debris from an earlier ceiling above
    *   pipe insulation, either damaged or debris from a poor strip
    *   spray coating on steel work, again either damaged or debris from a poor strip.

Access into ceiling voids must be done very cautiously, if at all. Account must be taken of the age of the building and any records of refurbishment or replacement of suspended ceilings.

**Fig 8.3** A typical example of a new ceiling installed beneath (and attached to) the original asbestos ceiling

General instructions for access into the various types of ceilings can then be as follows.

## MMMF – "drop in" tiles

Place a polythene sheet on the floor under the step-ladder to catch any debris which may be released when removing tiles. Have a HEPA Type H vacuum cleaner and wet wipes available to clean up any debris. The surveyor must wear suitable RPE and PPE. Remove the ceiling tile very carefully without tilting if possible, sliding it into the ceiling void. These tiles are usually very fragile and easily damaged.

## Asbestos tiles – "drop in" type

As for MMMF tiles, but great caution must be exercised when moving the tiles.

## *Asbestos tiles – screwed or nailed to wooden battens*

Access through these tiles will need to be considered very carefully. The screw heads will usually have been countersunk or recessed and probably filled as well. Where the tiles were nailed, it will be almost impossible to access the void without causing significant damage to the tile.

For a Type 1 or 2 survey, (unless the client is insistent) the ceiling void will have to be denoted as "no access". In this case, it will be even more important to get information from the desk-top study, and to emphasize to the client that the void may contain ACMs not otherwise identified.

Disturbing these tiles will need the services of a licenced contractor and if the number of tiles is more than two or three, it will be subject to full notification to the appropriate enforcing authority in accordance with the terms of the contractor's licence.

# Storage and labelling of samples

Note that MDHS 77 is equivocal about the procedure of double bagging and appears to allow a number of separate (single bagged) samples to be bagged together in another single container – this is NOT acceptable practice. MDHS 100 makes it quite clear that each single sample must be individually bagged and then double bagged.

The standard bags used by most surveyors are the self-seal polythene bags with white writing panels. These are readily available in bulk and are quite suitable. When sealing the bags, remove as much of the air as possible; otherwise the samples may occupy a rather large volume at the end of the sampling!

Each sample bag must be labelled as a minimum with a unique identifier but if possible also with a number of other pieces of information, including:

- unique identifying reference number
- date
- site
- building identity
- floor and room number

- sample location or description
- surveyors' initials.

Preferably both bags should be labelled in the same way with the same information. Alternatively, this information may be included (or duplicated) on the survey worksheets.

# Transport of samples

Usually, samples collected on site will need to be transported to a laboratory for analysis. It is common for the samples to be sent through the post. However, if the volume of the container exceeds 5 litres they are then subject to provisions of the Road Traffic (Carriage of Dangerous Substances in Packages etc.) Regulations 1992. The basic requirements include provisions for packaging and labelling, accompanying information on the nature of the materials and the associated hazards to which they could give rise.

The Post Office will not carry asbestos samples but there are certain carriers who are able to carry and deliver the samples in accordance with these regulations, and the best advice is to seek a specialist carrier.

In any case, it is prudent to notify the laboratory and label the package with some warning such as "To be opened under controlled conditions" or "For the attention of XXX".

# Archiving of samples

Laboratories that are accredited by UKAS for the analysis of bulk samples for asbestos must retain the samples for at least six months after analysis, so that if there are any queries the analysis can be rechecked. In any case, they may be re-analysed by the laboratory as part of their own internal quality control checks. There are no problems with the stability of the samples. They are not likely to decay or degrade in any way under normal storage conditions – but they must be stored in a manner which protects their integrity and prevents any contamination of the sample. They will need to be stored under controlled, not necessarily high security, conditions which mean that samples can be accessed only by authorised persons and retrieved with confidence.

Samples which are taken as part of a dispute or likely to be material evidence in litigation or in a prosecution must clearly be retained for much longer. In addition, it is then usual to use some form of documentation which ensures a chain of custody for the samples.

# Material Risk Assessments and Management Prioritisation

## Risk assessment algorithms

Regulation 4(8) of CAWR 2002 requires the dutyholder to assess the risk from the asbestos material located.

> (8) Where the assessment shows that asbestos is or is liable to be present in any part of the premises the dutyholder shall ensure that:
> (a) a determination of the risk from that asbestos is made

It is evident that friable asbestos thermal insulation on pipework in a plant room is a far greater hazard than the thermoplastic floor tiles in the corridor outside, and the dutyholder needs to take account of that difference. We then need to consider ways in which weighting can be given to various asbestos containing materials within a building.

This need has been recognised for many years, of course, and the great majority of organisations involved with asbestos surveying have used some kind of numerical scoring systems or algorithms to arrive at a ranking to assist the management of the asbestos. One local authority used something as simple as "satisfactory" or "not satisfactory" and this is not an acceptable approach.

The number of systems used (of varying complexity) was perhaps almost as many as the organisations involved with surveys. Certainly, experience of a number of local authorities up to 2001 showed that hardly any of them used the same system; most had variations on a theme. Some systems gave very much greater weight to a material containing crocidolite or to areas where children or young people are likely to be present.

This variation is very understandable. Each authority will have a different set of properties to manage (both in terms of age and use – corporate, education and domestic premises, for example) and different political priorities (and budgets) in managing them. A local education authority, for example, has a very different set of problems and priorities to, say, a chemical plant or refinery.

As a general rule, all the schemes have taken account of a number of more or less common factors, such as:

- material type
- friability (ie softness or dustiness)
- condition
- surface treatment
- location
- accessibility
- quantity
- asbestos type and/or content.

In this list some of the factors are related, of course. The product type determines, largely, its friability. The location will determine the accessibility and hence the likelihood of further damage or exposure to airborne fibres to workers or occupants of the area.

However, the risk assessment needs to take into account how likely people are to be exposed to asbestos because of human activities which may damage the material, so other factors will be important, such as:

- the normal activity and use of the area
- number of people using this area and how often
- whether maintenance activities will disturb the material and how often

Each parameter is usually given a set of bands and scored accordingly. The band scores are often weighted to give emphasis to particularly serious conditions such as the presence of debris or the presence of crocidolite in the material. The greater the hazard the higher the numerical value.

The total score for the material is then added together, although in some systems a multiplier is included, to emphasise a particular factor. The final score is then broken down into a set of three or four bands, to indicate the relative significance of the material, and to give the management some means of handling a problem. Clearly, a high score demands action very soon. The maintenance budget for any premises is limited and management needs to know what asbestos materials are in need of attention first and what can be left to sometime in the future. This kind of scoring helps to focus on priorities.

Two points need to be emphasized. First, the purpose of the scoring system is to give some kind of structure to the decision-making process so it is evident to everyone how the score (and decision) has been reached. The score is intended to prioritise the actions. However, the score does not dictate what action needs to be taken (if any) and there may be other factors which management will take into account when deciding what actions are needed. For example, a ceiling of asbestos insulating board tiles may be in very good condition and does not need to be removed yet. In the next few months, however, electrical rewiring and new network cabling are planned, which will be easier if the ceiling void can be accessed. Management therefore decide that as part of general refurbishment the ceiling is removed at a convenient period well before the works are planned.

Second, it is important to recognise that the result of the algorithm is not necessarily perfect. It will be influenced by subjective judgments about condition, for example, and may also be based on imperfect knowledge about some of the influencing factors. Adequate training of surveyors is needed to achieve consistency in interpretation and scoring.

(To illustrate the problem of subjective assessment, try getting a group of surveyors to assess the condition of some slightly damaged panels. Their scores will vary significantly, and will be influenced by their position as consultant/surveyor, removal contractor, maintenance manager or occupant/tenant.)

# MDHS 100 and HSG 227

It is evident that there are two principal considerations:

(a)  What sort of material is this and how likely is it to release fibres into the atmosphere?

(b)  What human/mechanical factors make it likely that people will be exposed to airborne fibres?

Most of the schemes prior to MDHS 100 would have taken these into account in a variety of ways and to different depths without distinction between these factors. MDHS 100 and HSG 227, however, introduced a clear separation between the two stages. The scoring system and its application are described in detail (with worked examples) in HSG 227 – *A comprehensive guide to managing asbestos in premises*.

These are referred to in HSG 227 as the "material assessment" and the "priority assessment". The sum of the scores for each assessment gives the overall risk assessment for the material.

# Material assessments

The assessment covers four factors:

* product type
* condition or extent of damage
* surface treatment
* asbestos type.

Each factor is scored up to three points (so could score a maximum score of 12 points). The scoring in detail is shown in Table 9.1 (adapted from HSG 227).

## *Explanatory notes*

### *Product type*

Decorative coatings are strictly a coating which contains asbestos and are therefore subject to the Asbestos (Licensing) Regulations 1983. However, because this is clearly a low concentration bonded material, it scores 1 under "product type".

**Table 9.1** Material assessment scoring

| Parameter | Example | Score |
|---|---|---|
| Product type | Sprayed coatings, thermal insulation, loose asbestos packing, asbestos mattresses, etc. | 3 |
| | Insulating board, millboard, ropes and textiles, gaskets, papers | 2 |
| | Cement products, plastics, resin or rubber based products, bitumen products, textured paints or decorative coatings | 1 |
| Condition or extent of damage | Serious damage or delamination; visible debris | 3 |
| | Medium damage. Significant breakage or several small areas of minor damage, a few loose fibres exposed | 2 |
| | Low damage. A few scratches, broken edges on boards or tiles | 1 |
| | No visible damage or deterioration | 0 |
| Surface treatment | Unsealed lagging or spray coatings | 3 |
| | Encapsulated lagging/sprays; unsealed insulating boards | 2 |
| | Enclosed lagging/sprays; sealed boards, unsealed cement products, paint sealed decorative coatings | 1 |
| | Composite materials, (reinforced plastics, resin-based or bitumen products), sealed cement sheets | 0 |
| Asbestos type | Crocidolite | 3 |
| | Amphibole asbestos (excluding crocidolite) | 2 |
| | Chrysotile alone | 1 |

## Extent of damage

Note the comments above regarding subjective interpretation. Training of surveyors to ensure consistent application is essential.

## Surface treatment

"Surface treatment" distinguishes between "encapsulated" or "sealed" on the one hand and "enclosed" on the other. "Encapsulated" or "sealed" means a paint or cloth coating; "enclosed" means a rigid covering of wood, metal or plastic (or even possibly with AIB or asbestos cement). However, unsealed insulation/spray scores 3, unsealed AIB scores 2 and unsealed AC scores 1. Additional encapsulation or enclosure for each material reduces the score by 1 or 2 points respectively. To illustrate this:

|  | Unsealed, bare | Encapsulated (Painted or sealed) | Enclosed |
|---|---|---|---|
| Spray coatings or Insulation | 3 | 2 | 1 |
| Insulating board | 2 | 1 | 0 |
| Cement products | 1 | 0 | 0 |

Textured coatings are not covered in the original MDHS 100 / HSG 227 scoring and this is an example of an interpolation.

## Asbestos type

The "asbestos type" in this system does not take concentration into account. Where there is a mixture, the highest type only is scored (eg insulating board with amosite and a small amount of chrysotile scores 2, but asbestos cement with chrysotile and a small amount of crocidolite scores 3).

The "asbestos type" may not be known until the sample analysis is completed. For a Type 1 (presumptive) survey, the asbestos type could be presumed if there were good justification to assume the composition normally expected for this type of material. Otherwise it would be assumed to contain crocidolite and score 3 points.

Just two very simple examples:

1. A crocidolite sprayed coating unsealed and with evidence of debris will score a total of 12 points.

2.  Floor tiles with chrysotile sealed and in good condition will score a total of 2 points.

The surveyor makes these assessments scores on site during the survey and sampling. The analysis is needed to confirm the identification.

If the result is that the material does not contain asbestos, obviously the whole assessment score defaults to 0. The material does not go on the register, but it will be important to record that the material has been sampled and confirmed to be asbestos-free.

# Priority assessments

The priority assessment takes account of the factors which are likely to result in disturbance and consequent exposure to airborne asbestos fibres.

The scheme covers four factors:

*   normal occupant activity
*   likelihood of disturbance
*   human exposure potential
*   maintenance activity.

Again, each factor is scored up to three points with a maximum total of 12 points. In this case it is a little more complicated because three of the parameters are averages of sub-assessments within the parameter.

In the case of "Likelihood of exposure", "Human exposure potential" and "Maintenance activity", the system requires sub-assessments to be made and then an average taken to arrive at the overall score for each parameter.

This scheme requires fairly detailed information to be available or for some general assumptions to be made. It is obviously not very easy to operate this on a paper record system – it is much more likely to be used as part of computer database type system where dropdown menu selection makes this very simple.

The initial discussions with the client will require that an agreement is reached on, firstly, what type of scoring system to use and, secondly, how much information is to be gathered by the surveyor and how much to be provided by the client.

The scoring in detail is shown in Table 9.2.

**Table 9.2** Priority assessment scoring

| Parameter | Example | Score |
|---|---|---|
| **Normal occupant activity** | High levels of disturbance (eg fire door with asbestos insulating board in constant use) | 3 |
| | Periodic disturbance (eg industrial or vehicular activity) | 2 |
| | Low disturbance (eg office type activity) | 1 |
| | Rare disturbance activity (eg little used store room) | 0 |
| **Likelihood of disturbance** | | |
| Location | Confined space | 3 |
| | Rooms up to 100 m$^2$ | 2 |
| | Large rooms or well-ventilated areas | 1 |
| | Outdoors – external | 0 |
| Accessibility | Routinely disturbed | 3 |
| | Easily disturbed | 2 |
| | Occasionally likely to be disturbed | 1 |
| | Usually inaccessible or unlikely to be disturbed | 0 |
| Extent/amount | >50m$^2$ or >50m pipe run | 3 |
| | >10m$^2$ to ≤50m$^2$ or >10m to ≤50m pipe run | 2 |
| | ≤10m$^2$ or ≤10m pipe run | 1 |
| | small amounts or items (eg gaskets or string) | 0 |
| **Human exposure potential** | | |
| No of occupants | >10 | 3 |
| | 4–10 | 2 |
| | 1–3 | 1 |
| | None | 0 |
| Frequency of use | Daily | 3 |
| | Weekly | 2 |
| | Monthly | 1 |
| | Infrequent | 0 |

| Parameter | Example | Score |
|---|---|---|
| Average time in use | > 6 hours | 3 |
| | >3 to <6 hours | 2 |
| | >1 to <3 hours | 1 |
| | <1 hour | 0 |
| **Maintenance activity** | | |
| Type of activity | High disturbance (eg removing asbestos ceiling tiles to replace a valve or for recabling) | 3 |
| | Medium disturbance (eg removing one or two asbestos ceiling tiles) | 2 |
| | Low disturbance (eg changing light bulbs in asbestos insulating board ceiling) | 1 |
| | Minor disturbance (possibility of contact when gaining access) | 0 |
| Frequency of activity | >1 per month | 3 |
| | >1 per year | 2 |
| | ≤1 per year | 1 |
| | unlikely to be disturbed for maintenance | 0 |

Adapted from HSG 227

# Worked examples

HSG 227 gives some good examples of how the scheme would work in a primary school, a chemical plant and a hospital.

To add to this, we can illustrate material in a sheltered housing block environment (even though regulation 4 does not strictly apply to tenanted domestic premises). Suppose that the survey has identified the following materials.

(a) Sprayed coating of amosite asbestos on steelwork in the tank room on the roof

The coating is in poor condition and unsealed, and there is slight damage and debris to be seen. The tank room is accessed mainly by the maintenance staff checking the water quality and occasionally for work on the pipework.

Material assessment score = 11 points (3+3+3+2)

(b)  Insulating board on timber frame as ducting around heating and hot water services in corridors throughout the block. There are eight of these risers.

The AIB is paint sealed but as it is exposed in the corridors, there is a small amount of accidental damage evident on some of the risers, where wheel-chairs and trolleys have knocked the box riser. Several panels have been cracked.

Material assessment score = 7 points (2+2+1+2)

(c)  Chrysotile thermoplastic floor tiles.

These are generally in good condition with very little evidence of deterioration. They are wet cleaned twice weekly and polished every three months.

Material assessment score = 2 points (1+0+0+1)

(d)  Chrysotile rope seal around the oven doors in the kitchen.

The rope seals are in very good condition, even though the equipment is now 15 years old.

Material assessment score = 5 points (2+0+2+1)

(e)  AC tiles to porch.

These are in perfectly good condition although now about 25 years old. The analysis shows they contain only chrysotile.

Material assessment score = 3 points (1+0+1+1)

The first point to note here is that these scores do make sense. The scores are clearly in order of importance and likelihood of fibre release. However, we now need to take account of other factors which will lead to people being exposed to airborne asbestos fibres, which is where the prioritisation comes into effect.

# Priority assessment scores

## (a) Sprayed coating in tank room

| Parameter | Example | Score |
|---|---|---|
| **Normal occupant activity** | Low disturbance activities | 1 |
| **Likelihood of disturbance** | | |
| Location | Confined space | 3 |
| Accessibility | Easily disturbed | 2 |
| Extent/amount | ≤10 m$^2$ or ≤10 m pipe run | 1 |
| | | Avg = 2 |
| **Human exposure potential** | | |
| Number of occupants | 1–3 | 1 |
| Frequency of use | Infrequent | 0 |
| Average time in use | >1 to <3 hours | 1 |
| | | Avg = 1 |
| **Maintenance activity** | | |
| Type of activity | Minor disturbance (possibility of contact when gaining access) | 0 |
| Frequency of activity | >1 per year | 1 |
| | | Avg = 1 |

Material assessment score  = 11 points
Priority assessment score  =  5 points  (1+2+1+1)
Total score  = 16 points

## (b) Insulating board on box riser in corridors

| Parameter | Example | Score |
|---|---|---|
| **Normal occupant activity** | Corridors in constant use but low level of activity | 2 |
| **Likelihood of disturbance** | | |
| Location | Corridors, open and well-ventilated | 1 |
| Accessibility | Routinely disturbed | 3 |
| Extent/amount | Estimate approx 20 m$^2$ in total | 2 |
| | | Avg = 2 |

| Parameter | Example | Score |
|---|---|---|
| **Human exposure potential** | | |
| Number of occupants | 35 residents and 4 staff (plus visitors) | 3 |
| Frequency of use | Daily | 3 |
| Average time in use | > 6 hours | 3 |
| | | Avg = 3 |
| **Maintenance activity** | | |
| Type of activity | Occasional painting – no disturbance for access | 1 |
| Frequency of activity | ≤1 per year | 1 |
| | | Avg = 1 |

Material assessment score = 7 points
Priority assessment score = 8 points (2+2+3+1)
Total score = 15 points

## (c) Thermoplastic floor tiles

| Parameter | Example | Score |
|---|---|---|
| **Normal occupant activity** | Corridors in constant use but low level of activity | 2 |
| **Likelihood of disturbance** | | |
| Location | Corridors, open and well-ventilated | 2 |
| Accessibility | Routinely disturbed | 1 |
| Extent/amount | Estimated 150 m² throughout the block | 3 |
| | | Avg = 2 |
| **Human exposure potential** | | |
| Number of occupants | 35 residents and 4 staff (plus visitors) | 3 |
| Frequency of use | Daily | 3 |
| Average time in use | >6 hours | 3 |
| | | Avg = 3 |
| **Maintenance activity** | | |
| Type of activity | Polished every three months | 2 |
| Frequency of activity | >1 per month | 2 |
| | | Avg = 2 |

Material assessment score   =   2 points
Priority assessment score   =   9 points  (2+2+3+2)
Total score                 = 11 points

## (d)  Asbestos rope seals on oven doors

| Parameter | Example | Score |
|---|---|---|
| **Normal occupant activity** | Periodic disturbance in normal use | 2 |
| **Likelihood of disturbance** | | |
| Location | Kitchen is approximately 60 m$^2$ | 2 |
| Accessibility | Easily disturbed | 2 |
| Extent/amount | Approximately 2 m length in total | 0 |
| | | Avg = 1 |
| **Human exposure potential** | | |
| Number of occupants | 2 staff | 1 |
| Frequency of use | Daily | 3 |
| Average time in use | > 6 hours | 3 |
| | | Avg = 2 |
| **Maintenance activity** | | |
| Type of activity | Major clean of kitchen equipment | 2 |
| Frequency of activity | 4 times per year | 2 |
| | | Avg = 2 |

Material assessment score   =   5 points
Priority assessment score   =   7 points  (2+1+2+2)
Total score                 = 12 points

## (e)  AC roof tiles to porch

| Parameter | Example | Score |
|---|---|---|
| **Normal occupant activity** | External – not normally disturbed | 0 |
| **Likelihood of disturbance** | | |
| Location | External | 0 |
| Accessibility | Unlikely to be disturbed | 0 |
| Extent/amount | Estimated about 4 m$^2$ | 1 |
| | | Avg = 0 |

| Parameter | Example | Score |
|---|---|---|
| **Human exposure potential** | | |
| Number of occupants | None | 0 |
| Frequency of use | Nil | 0 |
| Average time in use | Nil | 0 |
| | | Avg = 0 |
| | | |
| **Maintenance activity** | | |
| Type of activity | Minor disturbance to clear gutters | 1 |
| Frequency of activity | Annually | 1 |
| | | Avg = 1 |

Material assessment score = 3 points
Priority assessment score = 1 point (0+0+0+1)
Total score = 4 points

## Summary

| ACM | | Material Assessment score | Priority Assessment score | Overall risk Assessment score |
|---|---|---|---|---|
| (a) | Spray coating in tank room | 11 | 5 | 16 |
| (b) | Insulating board on box risers | 7 | 8 | 15 |
| (c) | Floor tiles in corridors | 2 | 9 | 11 |
| (d) | Rope seals on oven | 5 | 7 | 12 |
| (e) | Roof tiles | 3 | 1 | 4 |

The overall scores clearly place the emphasis on the sprayed coating in the tank room and the insulating board box risers. Of these, the spray coating is the highest risk material but in a location where few people are likely to be exposed to airborne fibres. The box riser has a lower material risk assessment but because it is in areas occupied by many people, the priority assessment score is higher.

The floor tiles are wet washed frequently but polished less often; the material assessment is very low but the priority assessment is higher than for the box riser because of the polishing. The rope seals are more likely to be disturbed but fewer people will be exposed, so the overall score is similar to that for the floor tiles.

Not surprisingly, the cement roof tiles score very low, and as we would expect, are not a great concern at this stage.

In these examples a degree of detail has been given here about the occupancy activities which may not normally be available to the surveyor and he/she will not necessarily be able to complete the whole risk assessment scoring. It will be necessary to reach an agreement as to which information can be put into the database by the surveyor and which will need to be inserted by the client.

# Alternative scoring schemes or algorithms

It must be stressed that the scoring system in MDHS 100 and HSG 227 is guidance only and not mandatory. UKAS would not necessarily require an accredited body to be using them if they had an equally satisfactory system that they preferred. Many organisations, however, have adopted this new system even though they were previously using another system. There is a benefit in using a common scheme so that a new employee or contractor immediately understands the scoring system.

From the client's point of view, of course, using the HSE's suggested scheme will help to demonstrate compliance with the legislative requirements.

It must be said that it is not the most "user-friendly" scheme and there are problems in achieving a degree of consistency in interpretation and application between different surveyors. If a surveyor and/or client wishes to use an alternative system, that will be entirely acceptable, provided that it is sufficiently flexible and gives an appropriate result at the end of the process.

# Analysis of Samples

This chapter is intended as an introduction to analysis for surveyors. It does not intend to provide anything like full training on the technique and aspiring analysts must seek out proper training courses such as the BOHS Proficiency Module P401. If science is a real turn-off and you do not need to do the identification of samples, skip this chapter. However it will still be useful as an introduction to the analytical method that is widely used for asbestos materials.

The technique of Polarised Light Microscopy (PLM) has long been widely used by mineralogists and geologists in the examination and identification of minerals so it makes perfect sense for this to be used for asbestos. The method, like any analytical technique has strengths and weaknesses. It is relatively cheap, quick and easy to set up, but it takes time and diligence to achieve proficiency and there are many pitfalls for novice analysts. For this procedure, experience is everything and even the most experienced of analysts will occasionally encounter a sample or material never seen before.

## Polarised light microscopy and dispersion staining – MDHS 77

The standard procedures now used by the vast majority of laboratories undertaking asbestos identification in the UK have been developed and refined over the last 30 years. The basic techniques are well established and have been used in optical microscopy to examine small particles in a variety of situations. It is not the purpose of this section to explain the finer details of the theory of the method but to provide the basic information needed by the surveyor. The basics of the method (and some theoretical background) are presented in MDHS 77 (now Annex II of the Analysts' Guide).

When the surveyor takes samples for analysis, he/she needs to have at least an appreciation of the analytical procedures although competence in analysis is not needed. There is a strong argument that it is helpful for surveyors to analyse the samples they take. The results provide feedback in learning to recognise the less common materials. Materials not previously encountered can surprise even experienced surveyors.

In practice, the present arrangement is that mostly surveyors cannot or do not, in the interests of efficiency, carry out the analysis. This is understandable – but a shame because experience shows that the most proficient analysts (in terms of speed and accuracy) are those who do a lot of analytical work. It is well recognised that proficiency in the method is all down to experience in seeing a wide range of materials. The analyst needs a good understanding of some of the underlying theory in order to interpret the observations that are not "textbook" and to understand what may (or may not) be acceptable variations.

## Equipment

The laboratory needs to be fitted out in a location to which access can be controlled, with easy to clean surfaces and floors, without carpets or carpet tiles. There needs to be access to running water and preferably at least basic laboratory facilities to allow some sample preparation techniques, such as acid washing, filtration, drying and crushing. All of these will need to be performed in a safe manner that does not contaminate other samples or unnecessarily expose anyone to asbestos.

The basic equipment consists of three items:

1. A suitable dust cabinet, fitted with a filtration system equivalent to the standard of a vacuum cleaner or air mover used in asbestos removal (ie to BS 5415 Type H). Ideally the unit should

vent externally, but if the exhaust air is recycled, there should be air testing on a regular basis (at least monthly) to confirm that the area is not being contaminated. Suitable cabinets are readily available off the shelf.

The front face will be glass or Perspex/polycarbonate and reduced aperture to ensure that the capture or face velocity is between 0.5 and 1.0 m/sec.

2. A low-power zoom stereomicroscope (7×–40× overall magnification) with suitable good quality adjustable illumination. The preferred type is a fibre-optic illuminator which can be located outside the cabinet. The stereomicroscope sits just inside the cabinet with the eyepieces protruding from the front.

3. A polarised light microscope (PLM) fitted with:
   - polariser and analyser filters
   - a first order red compensator (tint plate)
   - a McCrone Dispersion Staining Objective and/or phase contrast objective and phase contrast annulus for that objective.

The last two items (McCrone objective and phase contrast objective) are a matter of choice. The vast majority of analysts rely solely on the McCrone objective, but a few laboratories prefer the phase contrast system. The author's preference is to have both systems available to give maximum options in dealing with awkward samples.

In addition, the laboratory will need a supply of consumables such as disposable petri dishes, fine tipped tweezers, seekers (fine needles), Cargille liquids (refractive index liquids), tissues and wet wipes. A HEPA vacuum cleaner will be needed occasionally to clean up the cabinet, particularly after working with dusty samples.

The total cost of the system is about £10,000. It is important to choose a top-quality zoom stereomicroscope and with good-quality adjustable illumination. Do not choose a type with fixed magnification objectives as these will not give the flexibility needed. The examination of the sample under the stereomicroscope is the critical step in the analysis and as quite some time will be spent at the stereomicroscope, the benefits of the best quality will soon be obvious.

In contrast, the choice of the polarised light microscope (PLM) is not so critical and although a really good quality unit (Olympus BX series, for example) is highly desirable, units costing substantially less will be probably be quite adequate.

# Optical properties of crystalline materials

The method depends on the observation of a number of optical properties of the mineral fibres under polarised light. The results are combined and, although there may be a crucial observation or piece of evidence, it is the combination of information that provides the final answer. MDHS 77 requires all these observations to be made and the information recorded. MDHS 77 includes excellent colour illustrations of the observations for the various fibre types.

## Morphology and colour

The basic colour of the (clean) fibre and its appearance as observed under the stereomicroscope is important information to record. The morphology describes the appearance of the fibre – straight, springy, harsh, soft, elastic, shiny, undulose (wavy), etc.

## Birefringence

Birefringence occurs in materials where atoms are in regular arrays in a lattice type structure. In general, for a crystalline material, there will be three optical axes more or less mutually perpendicular (depending on the crystal structure). Strictly, the birefringence is defined as the numerical difference between the highest and lowest refractive indices and the birefringence will be classified as low, medium (moderate) or high. All the asbestos minerals are either low birefringence (chrysotile or crocidolite) or medium birefringence.

Birefringence is observed under crossed polars when the two refractive indices produce interference colours at angles away from the planes of polarisation (vertical or horizontal). The interference colours observed are normally low first order colours, through grey to white. In the case of crocidolite, because of the fibre's blue colour, these interference colours can appear as a brown, but varying in some cases from a pale brown to an intense, almost brick-red colour.

The colour is very variable from one sample of crocidolite to another, but is nevertheless highly characteristic. (These are referred to as "anomalous interference colours" because this brown colour does not appear in the normal series of interference colours).

## Optic orientation (sign of elongation)

The optic orientation describes whether the highest refractive index is along or across the fibre. Where the highest refractive index is along the fibre, it is referred to as "positive sign of elongation" or "length slow" (since the refractive index is inversely proportional to the speed of light in that axis).

It turns out that, of the asbestos minerals, all except crocidolite have a "positive sign of elongation" (or "length slow"). Even crocidolite, which is normally "length fast" – can (and does) appear as positive sign of elongation if it has been subjected to moderate heat above about 400°C. (Remember that the birefringence for crocidolite is very low and it does not take much heat to switch the crystal structure from "negative" to "positive".)

## Angle of extinction

The optical planes of the crystal do not necessarily coincide with the geometric planes of the fibre, and specifically in the case of tremolite and actinolite, the optical plane "along" the fibre is inclined to the fibre axis ("oblique") and this can be observed under crossed polars. These two are the only asbestos types to demonstrate this phenomenon. These two asbestos types are related in a "solid-solution series", where iron:magnesium ratio appears in a continuous series of compositions, depending on the source material. (Low iron compositions would be termed tremolite and higher iron content compositions would be termed actinolite).

## Pleochroism

Pleochroism is seen only in strongly coloured minerals such as crocidolite (blue) or actinolite (green). In effect, the absorption spectrum is different in different axes because of the arrangement of atoms in the lattice. The different colours (or a change of colour) can be observed with plane polarised light by aligning the fibre perpendicular and parallel to the plane of polarisation. Pleochroism may also be seen in amosite which has become thermally degraded, leading to oxidation of the iron in the crystal lattice, or in a thicker fibre (which may not be suitable for observing the other properties).

## Refractive index assessment by McCrone objective or by phase contrast

The refractive index of most materials is wavelength dependent: usually higher refractive index at the lower wavelength or blue end of the visible spectrum. When plotted against wavelength, the curve is referred to as the dispersion curve. The same property will be found in the refractive index liquids used (Cargille liquids) but these are often selected as "high dispersion" liquids, that is with a steeper slope of the dispersion curve than for the solid materials under investigation. To observe a refractive index match, a Cargille liquid is selected with the same (or very close) refractive index as suspected for the sample material. At some point in the visible spectrum, the two curves will intersect and the wavelength at the intersection is labelled $\lambda_0$. The intersection points ($\lambda_0$) for the fibre and liquid will be different for the two axes and can be seen as different colours corresponding to the two $\lambda_0$ wavelengths when viewed under plane polarised light.

Fortunately, most of the fibres possess rather different refractive indices, so the appropriate choice of liquid will give characteristic colours in the right liquid. In the "wrong" liquid, no colours will be seen. (If the mis-match is not too great, however, the colours can still indicate whether the fibre is of lower or higher refractive index than the liquid.)

The same properties are seen with the use of phase contrast but the intersection of the dispersion curves is now shown as a blue fibre with an orange-purple halo around the fibre. The appearance is quite different to that with the McCrone objective, but is just as characteristic. One advantage of phase contrast is that the presence of extraneous material (such as binder from insulation) is not so likely to obscure the fibre colours. A further advantage is that if the fibre is mounted in the "wrong" liquid, the appearance of the fibre immediately tells the microscopist whether the fibre is of lower or higher refractive index than the liquid. Fibres of higher RI appear darker than the background; fibres which are lower RI appear lighter.

Phase contrast is not widely used by laboratories in the UK for asbestos identification, which is a shame since it does have some very useful advantages. It should be said, however, that the colour illustrations in the original editions of MDHS 77 do not do full justice to the method and laboratories may not have really appreciated its value.

## Estimation of quantity

It must be very strongly emphasized that this method is qualitative and not quantitative. Any estimation of quantity is entirely subjective. Evidence shows that analysts tend to over-estimate quantity, particularly for chrysotile. Although clients sometimes want to put information on waste disposal consignment notes (and some survey risk assessments have included "concentration" as a parameter), many laboratories now will only record an estimate on the worksheet. On the final certificate they will report only those asbestos forms found – with no reference to quantity.

UKAS accreditation for asbestos identification will not cover estimation of quantity and they will therefore require a disclaimer on the certificate to show that the quantification is outside the scope of accreditation.

## Sample preparation techniques

In general, the method tries to keep sample preparation to a minimum. The major point is that samples need to be dry before slides are prepared, as water at the fibre-liquid interface will interfere with the dispersion effects. Fibres can be dried by rinsing with acetone and allowing the excess to quickly dry in air, or alternatively the sample can be allowed to air-dry in a partly closed petri dish at the back of the cabinet – this is tedious as no other samples can be analysed in the meanwhile.

The two main techniques used are:

• crushing with a pestle and mortar or breaking to extract fibres at the fracture

- acid wash.

The acid wash is often done with dilute hydrochloric acid (5M) for about 10–15 minutes at room temperature. It should be remembered that chrysotile is susceptible to strong acid attack so this treatment must not be overdone. After the treatment, the sample must be washed with water, filtered and rinsed with acetone to dry the sample.

Acid wash is a particularly effective technique for insulation samples, to remove the binder, and for cement samples which may contain traces of amphiboles. It is particularly useful for the material known as Wallboard D, a cement panel about 3 mm thick with wood fibre and a low content of chrysotile and possibly crocidolite. Some analysts have used acid wash for textured coating samples which are notoriously difficult to analyse.

Organic solvents may be used for bituminous materials (roofing felt, DPC, for example) although acetone may not be particularly effective – cyclohexane may be a better choice. (Avoid n-hexane, benzene and toluene, because of the health hazards, unless very well controlled conditions are available).

## *Thermal degradation*

The analyst will occasionally encounter samples of asbestos which have undergone changes through exposure to heat. This would typically be seen in samples which have been subjected to a fire, or in a situation where continuous high temperatures are experienced, eg a furnace, turbine, boiler or superheated steam line.

The asbestos fibres undergo a number of physical and chemical changes, which include:

- increase in refractive index (so the normal dispersion colours are changed). For the McCrone dispersion objective, if the RI shift is not too great, the colours seen may be indicative of a near match
- decrease in tensile strength. The fibres become very brittle and crumbly when the analyst tries to manipulate them in sample preparation for mounting on a slide
- change in colour, particularly for the iron-containing amphiboles, amosite and crocidolite. In both the iron forms iron oxides and a typical brown colour appears. In the case of crocidolite, it may eventually become an orange-brown colour because of the

formation of haematite. Because of the increase in refractive index, it is generally regarded as impossible to then distinguish between thermally degraded forms of amosite and crocidolite, and the analyst will usually report this as "suspected thermally degraded amphibole". In some cases it may be possible to find undegraded fibres which confirm the suspected analysis

• changes in pleochroism occur because of the change in colour of the mineral.

# Limitations of the method – fibres which mimic chrysotile

There are several fibres which can mimic chrysotile, and all of them are organic. The most well known are leather, polyethylene or polypropylene and spider's web. All of these should not deceive an experienced analyst, but can prove tricky for a novice.

The reason that these have been found to be problems is that they may be found in situations where chrysotile may be expected. Leather has been used as a gasket material, polypropylene has been used in cement products, and spiders' web may be found in ducts where asbestos insulation debris is likely to be found. All of these are organic, of course, and will burn in a flame.

The discrimination between anthophyllite and tremolite by this method is not easy. They share most of the optical properties discussed above but the only difference is the oblique angle of extinction which may be observed for tremolite, and the latter property is often difficult to observe. If tremolite is mis-identified as anthophyllite (and vice versa) this would not normally be regarded as a problem since the sample has been identified as an amphibole and the same control limits and waste disposal requirements apply for both. AIMS would not penalise a result of reporting one for the other.

# Sensitivity

The method potentially has great sensitivity (without delving into the deeper definitions of analytical sensitivity or limits of detection). MDHS 77 calculates that the limit of detection could be of the order of 1ppm (1 mg/kg) but in reality this depends very much on the matrix and the size of the sample and also on the degree of dispersion of the asbestos within the matrix. 1 ppm in a bonded matrix such as a small piece of floor tile is a very different matter to 1 mg of chrysotile in a 1 kg sample of contaminated land or soil sample.

Nevertheless, the method is potentially much more sensitive than other methods such as Infra-red spectroscopy or X-ray Diffractometry (XRD) where the limit of detection is of the order of 1%.

# Quality assurance

## Training

One of the principal components of any quality system is training. For this procedure, there is only one recognised training course and that is the BOHS Proficiency Module P401. As well as a multiple choice question paper, the analyst also needs to be able to demonstrate analytical competence by the satisfactory analysis of six AIMS samples (see below).

## Proficiency testing

Another central component of quality management is the demonstration of analytical competence through participation in an external proficiency testing scheme. Although there are others, the most relevant in the UK is the AIMS scheme run by the Health and Safety Laboratory in Sheffield. Participant laboratories are supplied with three rounds of four samples per year and the results are marked according to a scheme which penalises errors.

In the AIMS scheme there are three error levels:

- super-critical error (20 points)
- critical error (12 points)
- non-critical error (7 points).

For a detailed explanation of the scoring scheme, refer to the HSL through their web site at http://www.hsl.gov.uk.

The scheme penalises false positives (reporting asbestos types not present) as well as false negatives (failing to find asbestos types present). To achieve a satisfactory performance, a laboratory should score not more than 47 points as a rolling score over the last three rounds. 47 points sounds excessively generous but the "bar" is gradually being reduced to 39 points and eventually to 29 points.

One of the advantages of the AIMS samples is that they are validated samples – a mix of real materials and synthetic mixtures. The samples remain with the lab and they can be used for the laboratory's internal QC scheme and for training new analysts.

The AIMS scheme gives a good indication of proficiency. If the laboratory is still not accredited, a client could ask the laboratory about their participation in AIMS and ask for evidence of their performance.

## *Replicate analysis*

A laboratory will be expected to undertake replicate analysis of samples to check the original reported result. Usually a laboratory will pick out one or two samples per analyst per month for checking, depending on throughput.

The laboratory will also retain some well characterised samples for an internal QC scheme (old AIMS samples, for example) which analysts will usually be required to analyse at the rate of about two per month. The purpose of the internal QC scheme is to check proficiency on a more frequent basis than would be provided by the external AIMS scheme.

## *Accreditation*

From 21 November 2004, laboratories offering a service of asbestos identification need to be accredited by UKAS to ISO 17025. In terms of the law, the duty is on the client to ensure that the laboratory is accredited, but if the laboratory analysis is for their own organisation (but not, for example, as part of a survey for a client) the laboratory simply needs to demonstrate that they comply with the relevant paragraphs of ISO 17025 without going through the full exercise of gaining accreditation.

147

## Reporting of results

It is usual for laboratories now to report just the types of asbestos found without reference to quantity: see "Estimation of quantity" above. The laboratory must search for and report all types of asbestos found. It would not be acceptable to stop at crocidolite or amosite, and fail to carry on to identify any other asbestos types present.

For quantification, as mentioned above, many laboratories will only refer to the asbestos types found with no estimate of quantity. Some laboratories will indicate an estimate of quantity as "trace", "minor", "major" – or "trace", "significant", "substantial". The boundaries between the categories are rather diffuse. They depend entirely on subjective estimation of quantity – which it is well recognised is not at all reliable. Mostly quantities are serious over-estimates and particularly so for chrysotile.

# Instrumental methods

There are a number of instrumental methods which have been used, including:

- X-ray diffraction (XRD)
- Scanning or Transmission Electron Microscopy (SEM or TEM) with EDXA (Energy Dispersive X-ray Analysis)
- Infra-red spectroscopy
- Thermogravimetric Analysis (TGA) with Differential Thermal Analysis (DTA).

The only methods used to any real extent now are the first two. Both require some substantial laboratory equipment, costing in the order of £25k–£50k, highly qualified analytical staff and laboratory support services.

The analysis time for each of these methods is much longer than the conventional PLM method. An experienced analyst with PLM can process perhaps about 40–50 samples per day; although this is not possible or advisable if these are all textured coatings. The instrumental methods could perhaps process about 10 samples per day so the cost per sample (including analyst and equipment cost) is liable to be an order of magnitude greater than for PLM.

These two (XRD and SEM/TEM with EDXA) may be needed where

a legal case needs to be built or defended, as confirmation of results obtained from PLM. They would not be justified for routine samples where PLM is quite satisfactory. It should be said that in most cases, PLM analysis by an accredited laboratory is perfectly acceptable.

# Difficult samples

It is worth commenting that there are some materials which are particularly awkward to analyse by the conventional PLM method.

## *Textured coatings*

Chrysotile if present in textured coatings is usually of the order of 0.5–3% w/w and the fibres are short, fine and not usually distributed in clumps. It is often difficult to detect chrysotile by this method and some laboratories or surveyors will simply "presume" (and not sample) or take samples to be analysed by SEM or TEM with EDXA. It is also probable that the success of the analysis depends on the size of the sample. As discussed in chapter 8, a tiny sample of textured coating (because we do not want to disturb the decoration) may be very misleading.

A few years ago there was a "notorious" AIMS sample made up with 8% chrysotile and coated onto plasterboard. Even though it was about three times the normal concentration, 19% of the laboratories failed to find the chrysotile.

A major consultancy laboratory had four samples which had been reported as "no asbestos detected". When analysed by TEM with EDXA, chrysotile was found to be present. When the analysts were informed of this and asked to try and find the asbestos they were only successful in one out of the four samples.

There may well be developments in analysis of textured coatings, either using acid clean-up or by electron microscopy, but these samples and negative results may need to be treated with caution.

## *Floor tiles*

Again, in floor tiles sometimes the asbestos is very fine and well dispersed. Breaking the tiles may well reveal clumps of fibres at the fracture.

# Reports and Registers

## Survey reports and contents

It is clearly essential for the final report to be useful to the client. Apart from matters of accuracy and completeness, the report must be clear, unambiguous and readily accessible to those who need to use it.

Producers of reports will have different styles and emphases but the basic content should include the following:

(a) Management summary
Bullet points on scope, date, main findings.
Overall recommendations and conclusions.
Further actions.

(b) Introduction
Commissioning of survey (contract reference?).
Purpose (management, demolition, refurbishment).
Type of survey (1, 2 or 3).
Compliance with MDHS 100?

(c) Premises surveyed
Clearly identify scope of buildings surveyed.
Brief description of premises, age, etc, including photograph? (Include description of building structure type.)
When carried out, by whom, accompanied by whom?
Sampling at the time of survey or later?

(d) Survey procedures
Inspection basis, and access to which areas.
Reasons for "no access".
Means of identifying areas not accessible.
Any building elements not included/excluded from survey.
Sampling protocols and frequency.
Special means of access to "contaminated" areas?
Any air monitoring carried out (personal/static).
Confirm all waste disposed of as asbestos waste?

(e) Materials risk assessments (condition assessments)
MDHS 100, Consultancy protocols, client protocols?
Explain risk assessment scoring systems if necessary.
Prioritisation?

(f) List materials found/sampled/confirmed
Building number/room number/location, etc.
Materials risk assessment scores?

(g) Recommendations for remedial actions
Management actions?
Appendices
  • analytical reports (If subcontracted, state by whom?)
  • plans showing presence/extent of ACMs and sampling points
  • photographs of each ACM located (linked to the database and the material assessment)
  • risk assessment scores.

How much of the data and recommendations are included as appendices is a matter of choice, governed by the client's requirements and the size of the survey.

# Data transcription

It is crucially important to include procedures for checking transcription of data from the survey, which may be as raw handwritten site data, and analytical results into the final report and register. Experience shows that transcription errors are extremely easy to introduce so there must be some rigorous checking of data transcriptions.

Some survey systems are based on direct computer data entry on site into the survey software via hand-held or laptop computers, possibly including data entry via printed barcodes. The data is then downloaded by infra-red, wireless or hard-wired network link. Other possibilities include USB memory sticks. The technology is developing so rapidly that it is impossible to be prescriptive. Systems such as these minimise the potential for errors, but it is wise to be mindful of the IT maxim – "garbage in, garbage out".

Surveyors should evaluate survey software critically. It needs to be "user-friendly" and in any case, the surveyors may well take time to become accustomed to the software. It should be easy to check the raw data (and correct it on site if necessary).

(One early software system had disastrous flaws. Errors in data entry could not be checked until downloaded on to the main system and the system required repetitive entry of data regarding the site identification code, building reference, floor and room number for each asbestos item located. The surveyors nearly mutinied.)

# Hard copy vs database registers

Survey reports are produced either as hard copy printed material or stored in electronic form, particularly since they may need to be consulted by contractors or maintenance staff who do not have access to an intranet, for example. Almost certainly the final report and register will be in some kind of electronic form since that is how it will have been produced in the first place. Whether it is transmitted to the client in electronic form is another matter to be agreed with the client.

As a general rule, large multi-site organisations or multi-building sites will find that electronic storage works better, but where each building has its own premises manager, they will need access to the information on their building.

# Hard copy registers

*Advantages*

Easy to consult for contractors
and staff on site

Specific document for each building

*Disadvantages*

Difficult  for many people to access
information

Cannot be incorporated easily into an
overall asset management system

Not easy to update data records as
buildings are refurbished and asbestos
removed

Plans and other information (analysis
results and risk assessment scores)
may be in different parts of the report

Not so easy to include photographs of
the ACM

# Database/electronic registers

*Advantages*

Easy to record data and risk
assessments as survey is carried
out – data entry can be more easily
verified

Easy access for many contractors
and site management can print off
specific information

Easy to include audit trail to verify
contractors have consulted register

Simpler management of multiple
building sites or multi-site organisations

Easy to link CAD plans and data
information, pictures, analysis results
and risk assessment scores

Easy to update information as
buildings are maintained and
refurbished.

Can extract summary information
easily for a group of buildings

Easy to include condition
re-assessments

*Disadvantages*

Access to register will be difficult
without access to intranet

Concerns about IT security

Concerns over long term data storage
with change in IT systems and
software

The balance of advantages and disadvantages clearly demonstrates why most surveys are based on electronic storage.

There are several proprietary commercial software packages available which may be freestanding or incorporated into an asset management package. The complexity of each depends on the scale of the operations and one system may well not be suitable for each survey.

Some of the most well-known systems include

- "MasTec" from Xaracon    (http://www.xaracon.com)
- Envacs    (http://www.envacs.com)
- PSI    (http://www.psi2000.com)

Having offended those (many others) not mentioned here, it must be said there are many others, with a range of scope and capabilities. For IT literate surveyors, it is not too difficult to write a suitable Microsoft™ Access database for a register.

Each package will probably be more suitable to some kind of surveys than to others and each will have its strengths and weaknesses. It is probably true to say for each of the commercial packages it will be possible to find equal numbers of users for and against the package they use. All it means is that the user must evaluate the package very carefully before committing themselves to it.

# Plans and CAD systems

It is essential that plans are available to show the location, extent and type of ACM in the building. Again, a number of packages are available, which can include isometric drawings to include risers and partitions. Some asset management packages allow the inclusion of the asbestos database as a separate "layer". One commercial package which has been used is "Archibus", in a very complex multi-building site and across a number of sites throughout the UK.

# Recommendations for remedial work

These are discussed again in chapter 12. It is worth repeating that a surveyor will be able to make fairly obvious recommendations about repair or removal of damaged asbestos but it will be necessary to allow the client to adopt other recommendations in the light of their own future management programmes.

For example, some asbestos material may be in reasonable condition and can be repaired. The client, on the other hand, knows that a major refurbishment programme is coming up in 18 months time, so this is a good time to remove the material as "enabling works". (It may be more likely, however, that a client will want to defer some repairs which the surveyor thinks are urgent but prefers to delay them because of the impending refurbishment.)

The surveyor should be prepared to discuss recommendations for remedial work with the client. Decisions from the surveyor will need to be made on site, since it will be difficult to make the decision with any accuracy in the comfort of the surveyor's office.

# Updating of registers

The choice of report format will be governed by the need to update registers as ACMs are removed or repaired. This is evidently easier with a computer database record because not all ACMs will be removed together.

The management plan will need to indicate who is responsible for updating the register and when. It will need to be done promptly, not at yearly intervals, for example, as contemplated by one organisation.

An out-of-date register could prove expensive. Examples have been seen where some asbestos removal work was commissioned in order to gain access for network cables through a partition that the register showed to be asbestos insulating board. When the contractor had built his enclosure and removed the panel, it was found to be labelled "asbestos free". Although the main partition was indeed asbestos insulating board, this particular panel had been replaced, but no one had updated the register. The consequence was unnecessary cost and delay in the works.

# Availability for maintenance and minor work

The client will need to consider how to make the survey information available to those who need it: maintenance staff, contractors or tenants/occupants. Is the register to be held at the premises? Or available through an intranet? One advantage of the computer-based systems is that an audit trail can be built in to check that a contractor has accessed the register to obtain the relevant information he needs.

In some cases, extracts from the register can be pulled out to add to a work instruction for maintenance staff to let them know whether there is asbestos in the premises and whether it will be likely to impact on their work – in which case, they will need to take suitable precautions.

For emergency work and repairs, the computer-based system potentially has advantages where a contractor can access the information even while the client management is not available for discussion. It clearly depends, however, on the ability of the contractor to have secure access to the intranet and the register.

As a "belt and braces" approach, therefore, it may be necessary to have both a computer-based system and a hard copy at the site. In this case, however, the contractor needs to be aware that the hard copy may not be the most up-to-date version.

# Asbestos Management Plans

The management plan is clearly the responsibility of the client, not the surveyor, unless they are surveying their own premises, of course. In the majority of cases, the surveyor is providing the initial basic information on which the client will build their management plan. The surveyor will not normally get involved with his plan, but it will be important for him to understand what the management plan is supposed to be achieving.

It should be emphasized at the outset that the new regulation 4 is a duty to manage, not a duty to survey, and certainly not a duty to remove asbestos. The survey is just a means to an end – and the objective is control and management of the asbestos to prevent persons being unnecessarily exposed to asbestos because of damage.

Surveyors are often asked to help with the preparation of a client's asbestos management plan. The plan, however, must be an integral part of the client's general management system. Any management plan for asbestos must be consistent with other systems the client uses to manage contractors. This management structure will be unique to the client and determined to a large extent by the operation and its structures. The surveyor (unless they are very close to the client organisation and understand its structures and in-house systems and procedures) will probably not have sufficient familiarity with the client's systems to be able to write a satisfactory asbestos management plan for them.

For the asbestos management plan to work effectively and efficiently, it needs to be devised and written by the client. The surveyor or consultant can help in explaining the objectives and providing basic information and services, but unless the plan is consistent with the client's systems it is unlikely to be able to be implemented properly and may be doomed to failure.

# Regulation 4 of CAWR 2002

In essence the dutyholder is required to decide whether asbestos is, or is likely to be, present in the premises and to assess the condition of any asbestos so found. (The initial assessment may not necessarily determine that a survey is necessary, if the building is relatively new.)

The dutyholder needs to record the assessment, review it at regular intervals and if there is evidence to suspect the assessment is no longer valid. There needs to be a written management plan which sets out how the risk is to be managed. It includes the requirements to re-inspect the ACMs, ensure they are kept safe and in sound condition, (or safely removed if needed) and to make available the information to maintenance staff and contractors who may disturb it, and to provide information to the emergency services.

The management plan must be reviewed at regular intervals and the management plan must be implemented.

## Definition of the "dutyholder"

The clear definition of the dutyholder caused some initial problems with the first consultative document (CD159) because of the different roles and responsibilities of employers, whether they may be tenants, leaseholders, freeholders, landlords, facilities managers, etc.

Regulation 4 is now quite clear that the dutyholder is that person or organisation responsible for the maintenance of the fabric of the premises. The duties may be shared for different parts of the premises, such as common areas, plant rooms, external areas, etc. It is important to recognise that the management of the asbestos is the crucial requirement, a survey simply is there to enable the management plan to have good data to work with. Many clients will have been mistaken in thinking that what they really needed to do was to get a survey done, only then to realise that the major part of the requirement is the management of that asbestos. In practice, more effort and resources will be needed for the management plan than the survey. The survey is simply the enabling step.

Many dutyholders will find the prospect of the management plan daunting in terms of time and resources, and the mere presence of asbestos in their premises is likely to be an emotive subject with employees or tenants. In managing the asbestos, it may simply appear to be "an accident waiting to happen" with all the additional costs of repairs, potential prosecution by the HSE, claims for compensation, insurance liabilities, damage to industrial relations, public image or relations with tenants. Dutyholders then may feel that a phased removal programme is the best solution, to get rid of the problem altogether (although it may actually never be possible to get rid of the problem until the building is demolished!). There is evidence that some organisations are already taking this approach – but this is not what the HSE are advocating.

# Management vs removal

The HSE have always maintained that the best approach for asbestos in sound condition and not likely to be damaged is to leave it well alone, protect it and manage it to prevent damage and exposure to asbestos.

Removing the material will inevitably leave airborne fibre concentrations within the building, perhaps for several months, during which the occupants will be exposed to asbestos. The HSE could not ask for all asbestos to be removed within a fixed period – the costs would be enormous (the asbestos removal resources and expertise would be stretched to breaking) and the waste disposal capacity would either not be available or extremely expensive. The total removal would have to be justified with a cost benefit analysis or Regulatory Impact Assessment (RIA), balancing the lives and attendant costs saved against the cost of removal. The RIA for regulation 4 was difficult enough: total removal would be very hard to justify.

There are, however, situations where asbestos will have to be removed and these can be broken down as follows:

- ACM is beyond economic repair
- ACM is in a vulnerable location where further damage is likely to occur
- a change of use of the area will make the ACM more vulnerable

- refurbishment of the area is planned and the ACM will need to be disturbed
- demolition of the area is planned.

## Remediation options

The basic options open for the management of ACMs include:

- no action required; keep material in good condition; prevent damage
- clean up any debris from small amounts of damage; repair and seal with paint or a proprietary sealant
- prevent access by putting the area out of bounds or locking and controlling access with a permit system
- physically protect the ACM with a hard layer, such as metal, plastic or wood, and, finally
- remove the ACM under controlled conditions.

Labelling of the asbestos will be considered later but it must be recognised at the outset this has limited usefulness and must not be considered unless other adequate controls have reduced the risk to acceptable levels already.

The surveyor will wish to make some recommendation to the client about remedial works but it must be emphasized that the client will have their own agenda, and there will be factors to take into consideration which the surveyor will have no knowledge of. The dutyholder/client will need to take their own decisions about remedial work, but clearly the surveyor will wish to advise (and must do so) if they regard a client's decision as not complying with the regulations and guidance.

# Repair and maintenance of ACMs
## Licensable materials

A licenced asbestos removal contractor will be required for any work on the three groups of ACMs.

- Sprayed coatings (including decorative or textured coatings).

- Insulation to pipe work or vessels.
- Insulating board.

Two important provisos are first, paint sealing insulating board in good condition may be carried out by an unlicensed contractor, but, second, work (removal or disturbance) of textured coatings containing asbestos will need the services of a licenced contractor.

Encapsulation of coatings or pipe insulation will also normally be required to be done by a licenced contractor under controlled conditions and within the requirements of their licence conditions.

For more details on licensable materials and activities, consult the HSE's *Guide to the Asbestos (Licensing) Regulations 1983* (L11).

## Non-licensable materials

Work on all other materials, such as:

- asbestos cement
- plastics, rubbers, floor tiles or other bonded materials containing asbestos
- gaskets, rope or textiles
- bitumen based products such as roofing felt
- mastics or adhesives with asbestos

do not need the use of a licenced contractor. However the work will still be subject to the requirements of the CAWR 2002. In particular, this will require a suitable risk assessment and plan of work to protect the operatives and leave the area clean. It will also require the disposal of any waste asbestos materials as special waste. (Some organisations, however, have a policy that any work on asbestos materials, licensable or not, will be done by a licenced contractor.)

## Labelling of ACMs

In many situations the client will wish to label asbestos materials as such, if that is their corporate policy.

Not every client will feel so enthusiastic about labelling asbestos, particularly if the premises are open to clients, members of the public or tenants. In these situations, however, it might be argued that there is a stronger case than ever for making sure that people realise this material is asbestos and must not be disturbed. It is, of course, such an emotive issue that one can well understand their reservations.

There can be great sympathy for not wishing to label a tenant's sitting room ceiling with an asbestos textured coating – that is hardly a sensitive or friendly approach to the tenant. On the other hand, labelling an asbestos cement panel under a classroom window in a school is inviting trouble if the occupants know (and they usually do) that any damage means that the classroom will be closed for a week while the panel is removed or repaired.

It must be clearly understood that labelling ACMs is just part of the management plan and not the major or principal control over the material. Labelling does not control the ACM or prevent actions which might damage it. There are a number of problems with labelling and the most common are these:

(a)  Labels fall off, get removed, covered over, hidden
    Removal is a common problem, perhaps where the occupants (the Chief Executive in one case) think that they spoil the décor and are not befitting the corporate style.

    If a label is missing because it has been removed (or was never labelled in the first place) a maintenance operative or contractor may be lulled into believing that the material is not asbestos. If some Asbestolux panels in the area have been removed but others still remain, this is clearly an accident waiting to happen.

(b)  Labels are painted over
    This is seen all too often. Decorators don't seem to realise what they are painting over.

(c)  Labels get ignored by maintenance operatives or contractors
    They usually have a set time to get a job done. They have tunnel vision and they don't want to waste time with anybody else interfering. ("After all, it's only one bit of asbestos, isn't it?")

(d)  Labels only refer to the immediate area
    This tile is labelled. What about the tile next to it, which isn't labelled? Commonsense tells you it is asbestos also, but commonsense may be in short supply when a job needs to be done quickly.

Any label should comply with the requirements of the Health and Safety (Signs and Signals) Regulations 1996, and so should be of a recognised and recognisable format. The normal sign for asbestos materials is the "a" logo as reproduced in the CAWR and many of the accompanying guidance documents from the HSE.

Some clients are tempted to use innocuous labels where the areas are open to public access to avoid alarming them. If the labels do not convey the meaning required then they may fail to alert the person to the fact that this material is asbestos and it has failed in its objective. For example, what does a little orange triangle mean? In any case, non-standard labels are subject to the same weaknesses as for standard labels.

Labels will need inspecting periodically to ensure that any labels supposed to be on ACMs are indeed present, not painted over, still legible and securely fixed. This may not be a problem, of course, and indeed can easily be incorporated into the routine condition re-assessment.

As a summary, labels must be a part of, not instead of a proper management system. Provision of information to maintenance operatives and contractors is vital.

# Provision of information to staff, contractors and visitors

This is a fundamental duty under regulation 4. How this is accomplished is a matter for the dutyholder. The dutyholder may need to demonstrate that the information has in fact been supplied to a contractor or maintenance staff member through a permit-to-work system, or an audit trail on the intranet to demonstrate that the information has been accessed (and when) by the appropriate person.

As an extension to this, it will be essential to ensure that everyone understands the way to access the information, and to understand any limitations on the scope of the information (ie based on which type of survey, Type 1, 2 or 3?)

# Re-inspection of ACMs

The re-inspection of ACMs needs to be done – according to guidance in the ACoP L127 – "as a minimum, every six to 12 months..." In fact the ACoP also indicates that the inspection period should be related to the likelihood of the material becoming damaged, because of occupancy activities, the type of material and its original condition. More friable and vulnerable materials should be inspected more frequently than bonded materials in a remote location.

This re-inspection could therefore be dictated to an extent by the prioritisation scores from MDHS 100 and HSG 227. If these are in the register database, it is a very simple matter to extract the re-inspection schedule.

The re-inspections do not need to be done by a qualified or certified surveyor. The dutyholder or his staff, if suitably experienced and competent, are perfectly able to do these inspections. The only concern is that people doing the re-inspections should achieve a degree of consistency in their judgments.

# Review of Management Plan

The dutyholder needs to review the effectiveness of the management plan and the guidance in L127 is that this should be done, as a minimum, every six months. The purpose is to determine whether the management plan is still working, is still appropriate and that staff are implementing the plan fully and correctly.

# Professional Matters 13

## Membership of professional organisations

Membership of professional organisations amongst the asbestos surveying fraternity is only a requirement for Chartered Surveyors and Occupational Hygienists. The vast majority of practising asbestos surveyors do not belong individually to professional bodies of any description, and if they do, it is usually incidental to their asbestos work.

The legislation and guidance does not require surveyors to be members of any professional body. Passing the BOHS P402 qualification gives a route to membership of BOHS if they wish, but not necessarily to the Faculty of Occupational Hygiene, for which they would need a higher qualification. Even P402 is not strictly necessary as membership of BOHS is open to anyone who is interested in the field of Occupational Hygiene.

## Sharing of information and experience

One of the interesting clauses in EN 45004, however, is clause 16. This requires accredited inspection bodies to share information and good practice (subject to commercial confidentiality) as part of their quality management system. This can be either through professional bodies (such as BOHS or RICS) or through ad hoc discussion groups.

Many asbestos surveying organisations, for example, are also members of the Asbestos Removal Contractors Association (ARCA) either as full or associate members – or members of ATaC (Asbestos Testing and Consultancy) which is the consultancy branch of ARCA.

Historically, the asbestos consultancy sector has been very isolationist. They have not readily talked to each other, let alone trusted each other. They feel they have been at the mercy of the more street-wise, stronger and commercially cute contractors for too long.

HSE have provided seminars for the asbestos laboratories – mainly those involved with fibre counting and identification, but these occur only every two years and have not yet touched on the subject of surveys.

ARCA, to their credit, have sponsored and supported the development of ATaC, but it has limited membership. Many laboratories refuse to have anything to do with ATaC because they see it as connected with ARCA (which it is, of course) and they perceive this as a conflict of interest with the removal contractors. HSE would certainly like to see some kind of communication between laboratories which exchanges information and leads to enhanced standards but it seems this is not going to be the forum.

BOHS have recently set up a SIG on fibres. Strictly speaking, its remit includes other industrial fibres such as glass fibre, refractory ceramic fibres, mineral wools and organic fibres such as Kevlar (p-aramid fibres), but clearly asbestos is the main interest of today. Since all the laboratories and many surveyors need BOHS qualifications they immediately have a connection and BOHS is seen to be independent of HSE and UKAS. Although surveying organisations may not like BOHS, maybe BOHS can provide the forum that would be beneficial to asbestos surveyors.

# Continuous Professional Development

RICS for some time now has required evidence of continuing professional development and BOHS has started to apply the same requirements for their Occupational Hygienists. Unfortunately, this does not apply to 99.9% of the asbestos surveyors working in the field.

# Professional Indemnity cover

One of the biggest problems faced by the asbestos industry, and specifically by the asbestos removal contractors, is the problem of insurance cover. Asbestos reinsurance cover for the American market wrecked the Lloyds "Names" in the 1990s and since then, the insurance industry has taken fright over asbestos. Employers liability cover costs for asbestos work have rocketed. Some contractors have gone out of business because of the increased insurance costs and new contractors are finding it extremely difficult to get adequate levels of cover because the insurance industry has limited amounts of cover available for the industry as a whole. The cost of asbestos removal has therefore increased as the insurance costs are passed on to the client.

Asbestos surveyors require professional indemnity cover. At one stage it looked as though this was going to be a serious problem, but some good negotiation with the insurance industry has led to deals available for surveyors who are certified by either of the two main schemes, ABICS or NIACS. Nevertheless, the same difficulties of finding adequate insurance cover affects surveying organisations as much as the contractors. The principal problem, of course, is the difficulty of finding every last piece of asbestos in a Type 3 survey – and the consequences of failure can be very expensive in terms of delays and extra costs. Those costs will have to be laid at someone's door and that door is likely to be the surveyor's, and his insurer, if he has one.

Any surveyor who operates without adequate PI cover is taking a great risk. There is a great fear within the industry at the moment that "cowboy" surveyors will step into the market and operate without the required cover with a consequent commercial advantage in reduced operating costs.

Insurance cover is without doubt the most intractable of problems for the asbestos surveying industry at the present time.

# Appendix: Abbreviations

| | |
|---|---|
| ABICS | Asbestos in Building Inspectors Certification Scheme |
| AC | Asbestos cement |
| ACMs | Asbestos Containing Materials |
| AIB | Asbestos Insulating Board |
| AIC | Asbestos Information Centre |
| AIMS | Asbestos in Materials Scheme (run by the Health and Safety Laboratory) |
| ARCA | Asbestos Removal Contractors Association |
| ATaC | Asbestos Testing and Consultancy (division of ARCA) |
| BCS | British Calibration Service |
| BOHS | British Occupational Hygiene Society |
| CAF | Compressed Asbestos Fibre |
| CDM | Construction (Design and Management) Regulations 1994 |
| DTA | Differential Thermal Analysis |
| DTI | Department of Trade and Industry |
| EDXA | Energy Dispersive X-ray Analysis |
| ERM | European Reference Method |
| FOH | Faculty of Occupational Hygiene |
| FRIB | Fire retardant insulating board |
| HPA | Health Protection Agency |
| HSE | Health and Safety Executive |
| HSWA | Health and Safety at Work etc Act 1974 |
| ISO | International Standards Organisation |

| MDHS | Methods for the Determination of Hazardous Substances |
| MHSAW | Management of Health and Safety at Work Regulations 1999 |
| MMMF | Man made mineral fibre |
| NIACS | National Individual Asbestos Certification Scheme |
| NAMAS | National Measurement Accreditation Scheme |
| NATLAS | National Testing Laboratory Accreditation Scheme |
| PFA | Pulverised Fuel Ash |
| PHLS | Public Health Laboratory Service now Health Protection Agency |
| PLM | Polarised Light Microscopy |
| PPE | Personal Protective Equipment |
| RIA | Regulatory Impact Assessment |
| RICS | Royal Institute of Chartered Surveyors |
| RIDDOR | Reporting of Injuries, Diseases and Dangerous Occurrences Regulations 1995 |
| RPE | Respiratory Protective Equipment |
| RPM | Robinson's Profiled Metal |
| SEM | Scanning Electron Microscopy |
| SI | Statutory Instrument |
| TEM | Transmission Electron Microscopy |
| TGA | Thermogravimetric Analysis |
| XRD | X-ray Diffraction Spectrometry |
| UKAS | United Kingdom Accreditation Service |

# Bibliography

**Documents available from HSE Books (T: 01787 881165 or http://www.hsebooks.co.uk)**

L127    The management of asbestos in non-domestic premises. Approved Code of Practice
        ISBN 0 7176 2382 3    £9.50

L27     Work with asbestos which does not normally require a licence. Approved Code of Practice
        ISBN 0 7176 2562 1    £9.50

L28     Work with asbestos insulation, asbestos coating and asbestos insulating board. Approved Code of Practice (4th ed 2002)
        ISBN 0 7176 2563 X    £9.50

L11     A guide to the Asbestos (Licensing) Regulations 1983
        ISBN 0 7176 2435 8    £6.00

HSG 227 A comprehensive guide to managing asbestos in premises
        ISBN 0 7176 2381 5    £12.50

INDG 288 Selection of suitable respiratory protective equipment for work with asbestos
        ISBN 0 7176 2220 7    (single copies free)

MDHS 39/4  Asbestos fibres in air
ISBN 0 7176 1113 2    £5.00

MDHS 77    Asbestos in bulk materials
ISBN 0 7176 0677 5    £11.50

MDHS 100   Surveying sampling and assessment of asbestos
containing materials (2001)
ISBN 0 7176 2076 X    £18.00

HSG xxx    Analysts Guide (to be published late 2004)

EH 10      Asbestos: exposure limits and measurement of airborne
dust concentrations (2001)
ISBN 0 7176 2129 X    £5.00

EH47       The provision, use and maintenance of hygiene facilities
for work with asbestos insulation, asbestos coatings and
asbestos insulating board (2002)
ISBN 0 7176 2299 1    £5.00

EH 51      Enclosures provided for work with asbestos insulation,
coatings and asbestos insulating board (2000)
ISBN 0 7176 1700 8    £10.00

## Documents from ISO  http://www.iso.org

ISO/IEC 17025:1999
General requirements for the competence of testing and calibration
laboratories

ISO/IEC 17020:1998
General criteria for the operation of various types of bodies
performing inspection

ISO/IEC 17024:2003
Conformity assessment – General requirements for bodies operating
certification of persons

# Index